EDUCATION POLICY ANALYSIS

2003

ORGANISATION FOR ECONOMIC CO-OPERATION AND DEVELOPMENT

The *Education Policy Analysis* series forms part of the work programme of the OECD Education Committee and the Directorate for Education. It is a collaborative effort between member governments, the national experts and organisations working with the OECD, and the OECD Secretariat The series is prepared by the Education and Training Policy Division under the direction of Abrar Hasan, and draws on a range of activities in the Directorate. The principal contributions to the 2003 issue were made by Phillip McKenzie and Donald Hirsch as editors, Peter Evans and Marcella Deluca (Chapter 1), Richard Sweet (Chapter 2), Kiyong Byun and Richard Yelland (Chapter 3), and Gregory Wurzburg (Chapter 4). Manuela De Sousa provided statistical support for Chapter 4; Georges Lemaitre provided advice. Co-ordination and copy editing were the responsibility of Delphine Grandrieux. Fung-Kwan Tam was responsible for graphic design. Dianne Fowler was responsible for administration. Colleagues in the OECD Secretariat provided helpful comments on initial drafts. Valuable comments on draft chapters were provided by national representatives on the OECD Education Committee, members of the Governing Board of the Centre for Educational Research and Innovation (CERI), national co-ordinators of the Indicators of National Education Systems (INES) project, and their colleagues. The views expressed in the published chapters, however, do not necessarily represent those of OECD member governments.

This report is published on the responsibility of the Secretary-General of the OECD.

ORGANISATION FOR ECONOMIC CO-OPERATION AND DEVELOPMENT

Pursuant to Article 1 of the Convention signed in Paris on 14th December 1960, and which came into force on 30th September 1961, the Organisation for Economic Co-operation and Development (OECD) shall promote policies designed:

- to achieve the highest sustainable economic growth and employment and a rising standard of living in member countries, while maintaining financial stability, and thus to contribute to the development of the world economy;
- to contribute to sound economic expansion in member as well as non-member countries in the process of economic development; and
- to contribute to the expansion of world trade on a multilateral, non-discriminatory basis in accordance with international obligations.

The original member countries of the OECD are Austria, Belgium, Canada, Denmark, France, Germany, Greece, Iceland, Ireland, Italy, Luxembourg, the Netherlands, Norway, Portugal, Spain, Sweden, Switzerland, Turkey, the United Kingdom and the United States. The following countries became members subsequently through accession at the dates indicated hereafter: Japan (28th April 1964), Finland (28th January 1969), Australia (7th June 1971), New Zealand (29th May 1973), Mexico (18th May 1994), the Czech Republic (21st December 1995), Hungary (7th May 1996), Poland (22nd November 1996), Korea (12th December 1996) and Slovak Republic (14th December 2000). The Commission of the European Communities takes part in the work of the OECD (Article 13 of the OECD Convention).

The Centre for Educational Research and Innovation was created in June 1968 by the Council of the Organisation for Economic Co-operation and Development and all member countries of the OECD are participants.

The main objectives of the Centre are as follows:

- *analyse and develop research, innovation and key indicators in current and emerging education and learning issues, and their links to other sectors of policy;*
- *explore forward-looking coherent approaches to education and learning in the context of national and international cultural, social and economic change; and*
- *facilitate practical co-operation among member countries and, where relevant, with non-member countries, in order to seek solutions and exchange views of educational problems of common interest.*

The Centre functions within the Organisation for Economic Co-operation and Development in accordance with the decisions of the Council of the Organisation, under the authority of the Secretary-General. It is supervised by a Governing Board composed of one national expert in its field of competence from each of the countries participating in its programme of work.

Publié en français sous le titre :
Analyse des politiques d'éducation
ÉDITION 2003

© OECD 2003

Permission to reproduce a portion of this work for non-commercial purposes or classroom use should be obtained through the Centre français d'exploitation du droit de copie (CFC), 20, rue des Grands-Augustins, 75006 Paris, France, tel. (33-1) 44 07 47 70, fax (33-1) 46 34 67 19, for every country except the United States. In the United States permission should be obtained through the Copyright Clearance Center, Customer Service, (508)750-8400, 222 Rosewood Drive, Danvers, MA 01923 USA, or CCC Online: www.copyright.com. All other applications for permission to reproduce or translate all or part of this book should be made to OECD Publications, 2, rue André-Pascal, 75775 Paris Cedex 16, France.

TABLE OF CONTENTS

INTRODUCTION: Building stronger policy connections 7

Chapter 1
**DIVERSITY, INCLUSION AND EQUITY:
INSIGHTS FROM SPECIAL NEEDS PROVISION** 9
Summary 10
1. INTRODUCTION 11
2. EQUITY AND INCLUSION 11
3. INTERNATIONAL DATA ON SPECIAL NEEDS PROVISION 13
4. MAKING EQUITABLE EDUCATION WORK 24
5. CONCLUSIONS 28
References 30
Appendix: Allocations of categories of students with disabilities, difficulties and disadvantages included in country resource definitions 31
Data for the Figures 35

Chapter 2
CAREER GUIDANCE: NEW WAYS FORWARD 39
Summary 40
1. INTRODUCTION 41
2. CAREER GUIDANCE TODAY 41
3. WHY DOES CAREER GUIDANCE MATTER FOR PUBLIC POLICY? 43
4. FROM DECISION MAKING TO CAREER MANAGEMENT SKILLS:
   A POLICY CHALLENGE FOR EDUCATION 47
5. WIDENING ACCESS FOR ADULTS 51
6. CONCLUSIONS 53
References 54
Appendix: Career education in the school curriculum in OECD countries 56
Data for the Figure 57

Chapter 3
CHANGING PATTERNS OF GOVERNANCE IN HIGHER EDUCATION 59
Summary 60
1. INTRODUCTION 61
2. INSTITUTIONAL AUTONOMY 62
3. FUNDING 65
4. QUALITY ASSESSMENT 69
5. INSTITUTIONAL GOVERNANCE 71
6. INSTITUTIONAL LEADERSHIP 73
7. CONCLUSIONS 75
References 76
Appendix: Country details on aspects of university autonomy 77

Chapter 4
**STRATEGIES FOR SUSTAINABLE INVESTMENT
IN ADULT LIFELONG LEARNING** 79

Summary 80

1. INTRODUCTION 81
2. ADULT LEARNING: THE WEAK LINK IN THE LIFELONG LEARNING
   FRAMEWORK 81
3. EVALUATING ECONOMIC SUSTAINABILITY 84
4. IMPROVING FINANCIAL SUSTAINABILITY 92
5. CONCLUSIONS AND POLICY PRIORITIES 98

References 99

Data for the Figure 101

ANNEX: Recent education policy developments in OECD countries 103

Education Policy Analysis: Purposes and previous editions 111

List of Boxes, Figures and Tables

BOXES

Box 1.1	Development of international indicators on students with disabilities, learning difficulties and disadvantages	13
Box 2.1	Career guidance: Three long-standing approaches	42
Box 2.2	Career guidance: Using innovation to widen access	42
Box 2.3	Evaluating career guidance	44
Box 2.4	"Guidance-oriented" schools	50
Box 3.1	National universities incorporation plan in Japan	64
Box 3.2	Research funding in the United Kingdom	66
Box 3.3	University performance contracting in Finland	68
Box 3.4	National quality assessment agencies: Similarities and differences	70
Box 4.1	Internal rates of return	84
Box 4.2	What actually happens to the earnings of adult learners? Evidence from Canada	87

FIGURES

Figure 1.1	Students in compulsory education receiving additional resources for defined disabilities, as a percentage of all students in compulsory education, 1999	14
Figure 1.2	Percentages of students in compulsory education receiving additional resources for defined disabilities, by location, 1999	15
Figure 1.3	Students in compulsory education receiving additional resources for defined difficulties, as a percentage of all students in compulsory education, 1999	17
Figure 1.4	Percentages of students in compulsory education receiving additional resources for defined difficulties, by location, 1999	18
Figure 1.5	Students in compulsory education receiving additional resources for defined disadvantages, as a percentage of all students in compulsory education, 1999	19
Figure 1.6	Percentages of students in compulsory education receiving additional resources for defined disadvantages, by location, 1999	19

Figure 1.7	Number of students receiving additional resources in special schools as a proportion of all students by age, 1999	22
Figure 2.1	Percentage of upper secondary students in academic and vocational programmes who receive individual career counselling, 2002	49
Figure 4.1	Average annual earnings by educational attainment and whether obtained highest qualification in the 1993-98 period, 30-49 year-olds, Canada	87

TABLES

Table 1.1	Gender and disability: proportion of students in compulsory education receiving additional resources for defined disabilities who are male, by location, 1999	16
Table 1.2	Gender and learning difficulties: proportion of students in compulsory education receiving additional resources for defined difficulties who are male, by location, 1999	18
Table 1.3	Gender and disadvantages: proportion of students in compulsory education receiving additional resources for defined disadvantages who are male, by location, 1999	20
Table 1.4	The number and size of special schools in compulsory education	21
Table 3.1	Extent of autonomy experienced by universities	63
Table 3.2	New methods for allocating recurrent funding to universities: country examples	67
Table 3.3	New models of institutional governance: country examples	72
Table 3.4	Appointment of leaders of higher education institutions	74
Table 4.1	Rates of return to obtaining upper secondary and university degree qualifications: illustrative data for 40-year-olds, Canada	89
Table 4.2	Rates of return to obtaining upper secondary and university degree qualifications: illustrative data for 40-year-olds, who obtain a 50% reduction in study time through accreditation of prior learning, Canada	91
Table 4.3	Co-financing mechanisms: objectives, types of measures, and country initiatives	94

INTRODUCTION: Building stronger policy connections

There is widespread recognition that education cannot be considered in isolation from other key public policies. Stronger linkages are most commonly sought with labour market and social policies, but education is also seen as requiring closer connections with the health, science, and environmental policy areas, among others.

The need for closer policy connections was a major theme when the chief executives of OECD education systems met in Dublin in February 2003. They expressed concern that "education is often not sufficiently connected with other policy developments, and this has negative consequences in both directions". The chief executives also drew attention to the paradox that "while education is at the centre of the knowledge economy, it is not itself knowledge rich". They went on to conclude that "there need to be better strategies for knowledge production about education and better connections between researchers and practitioners".

These concerns are closely related. Fundamental to building better links between education and other policy areas is the education sector's capacity to clearly articulate its objectives, to demonstrate how these inter-relate with wider social and economic developments, and to identify and implement cost-effective policies and programmes.

Economic and social changes have required education to develop a broadened conception of its role. The goal of achieving lifelong learning for all reflects a commitment to see policy as a connected whole. Education is no longer viewed as being confined largely to the experiences of children and young people, but as an on-going process of skill and knowledge development extending throughout life, and taking place in a wide variety of formal and informal settings. This broadened scope necessitates much closer integration between education, labour and social policies – but also exposes the limitations of the current knowledge base about how to make that work.

The creation of a separate OECD Directorate for Education in September 2002 recognised the central role that lifelong learning now plays in public policy. It also provided an opportunity to review how the OECD's education programme can help meet the policy challenges ahead. Building on its analyses of the operations of the education sector itself, the programme is placing an increased emphasis on "policy interconnectedness": trying to improve understanding of the mutual benefits that can flow from closer connections between education and other key policy areas; and using the tools of comparative analysis to identify good international practice in this regard.

The analyses reported in this volume reflect this orientation. Chapter 1 examines the role of education in improving social cohesion by drawing on international data and experience with programmes for students with disabilities, learning difficulties, and disadvantages. Chapter 2 discusses the contribution that new approaches to career guidance can make to the functioning of education systems and labour markets in a lifelong learning framework. Chapter 3 reviews the experiences of OECD countries that are reforming higher education in ways that attempt to balance achieving national economic and social objectives with strengthening the sector's independence and dynamism. Chapter 4 analyses policy strategies to increase investment in adult learning, which it argues is the weak link in the lifelong learning framework.

Although the chapters indicate that OECD countries share a number of common policy objectives – including lifting education participation by disadvantaged groups, raising the quality of education outcomes, and making education systems more responsive to social and economic needs – there are large differences in the policies and programmes they have adopted. Such differences reflect differences in national contexts, institutional structures, political factors, and resource constraints. However, the policy differences also reflect genuine uncertainties about the appropriate ways forward.

The chapters draw attention to significant limitations in the current knowledge base. Many countries lack analyses that link different types of provision to outcomes for students with disabilities, difficulties and disadvantages (Chapter 1), or that show how well the current suppliers of career education services are serving demand (Chapter 2). There is little analysis available of the impact of new funding and accountability mechanisms in higher education (Chapter 3), or of strategies intended to open up learning opportunities for disadvantaged adults (Chapter 4).

A significant part of the OECD's mission is to work with member countries to help fill such gaps. One contribution to this comes from documenting the range of policy initiatives now underway, whether in the substantive areas covered by the four chapters in this volume, or through the Annex that summarises recent major policy changes across a wide range of education fields in OECD countries. The changes cover the spectrum from early childhood education, through to schooling, tertiary education, adult learning and workplace training.

Comparative analyses of national policies can help countries place their own approaches in a broader perspective, and suggest innovations that they can learn from. Comparative analyses of this sort can also raise questions about long-established practices. For example, Chapter 1 documents substantial differences among OECD countries in how they identify students with special needs and provide for them. The result is that similar types of students can have vastly different educational and social experiences from country to country. And yet, as the chapter shows, there is relatively little information in most countries about the long-term consequences of special needs provision in different settings.

The OECD's work on education indicators, research, and policy reviews is intended to help member countries strengthen the knowledge base in this and other key areas, and to provide a stronger platform for policy development. A major theme of the current programme is finding ways to build connections between education and other areas of socio-economic policy. This will be a feature of the OECD Education Ministers meeting in March 2004 when they discuss policy issues on which an international comparative perspective can add value.

October 2003

DIVERSITY, INCLUSION AND EQUITY: INSIGHTS FROM SPECIAL NEEDS PROVISION

Summary	10
1. INTRODUCTION	11
2. EQUITY AND INCLUSION	11
3. INTERNATIONAL DATA ON SPECIAL NEEDS PROVISION	13
3.1 Students with disabilities	14
3.2 Students with learning difficulties	16
3.3 Students with disadvantages	17
3.4 Provision in special schools	21
4. MAKING EQUITABLE EDUCATION WORK	24
4.1 Recognising and planning for diversity	24
4.2 Using accountability and evaluation for improvement	25
4.3 Professional development of staff	25
4.4 External support services	25
4.5 Within-school support services	26
4.6 Co-operation between schools	27
4.7 Parent and community involvement	27
4.8 School organisation and management – opportunities for whole school development	27
4.9 Curriculum development	28
4.10 Classroom organisation	28
5. CONCLUSIONS	28
References	30
Appendix: Allocations of categories of students with disabilities, difficulties and disadvantages included in country resource definitions	31
Data for the Figures	35

Education Policy Analysis © OECD 2003

CHAPTER 1

DIVERSITY, INCLUSION AND EQUITY:
INSIGHTS FROM SPECIAL NEEDS PROVISION

SUMMARY

OECD countries are committed to ensuring that their education systems are equitable for all students, which requires them to provide for groups with diverse needs. An important part of this task is to structure programmes for students with disabilities, difficulties, and disadvantages in a way that respects and protects these groups' rights. This does not have clear-cut implications for the distribution of resources, since for many disabled students, for example, no amount of resources could produce outcomes equal to those of their non-disabled peers. Thus while this chapter provides an extensive international analysis of the allocation of resources to various groups (including by gender and age), these are indicators of the extent to which countries engage in a process of pursuing equity, rather than measuring progress towards an objective, well-defined standard.

What we can do, however, is to identify some key conditions that allow this process to be taken forward. The first is to recognise and plan for diversity. An indicator of whether this occurs is how many students attend special schools: this varies greatly across countries, and where it is high, this is a sign of mainstream schools' failure to accommodate diverse needs. Among a range of other conditions identified in the later part of this chapter, some relate to what is going on inside the school system, such as staff development and co-operation among schools, while others cover external relationships such as accountability and community involvement. The different national approaches documented in this chapter open up important questions about what works best for different types of students. Reforms in OECD countries are allowing understanding to accumulate on how best to address these issues, yet much remains to be done.

CHAPTER 1

DIVERSITY, INCLUSION AND EQUITY: INSIGHTS FROM SPECIAL NEEDS PROVISION

1. INTRODUCTION[1]

Creating equitable provision for diverse student populations is a key feature of education policy in OECD countries. At the centre of this challenge lies the goal of inclusion, leading ultimately to improved social cohesion. Education systems are expected to play their part in these social aspirations and countries have initiated a range of approaches intended to contribute to them. In this regard Education Ministers have asked the OECD to:

"Review how education and training systems can increase their capacity to include all learners and to achieve equitable outcomes for all, while meeting the increasing diversity of learners' needs, maintaining cultural diversity and improving quality." (OECD, 2001a, p.5)

This chapter is intended to contribute to this task by drawing on international data and experience based on programmes for students with disabilities, difficulties, and disadvantages. As well as documenting the wide variety of country approaches, it makes two main arguments: (i) a "rights-based" conception of equity implies that, wherever possible, these students should be educated in regular, mainstream schools rather than in separate institutions; and (ii) the various national approaches to including students with disabilities in regular schools provide useful lessons for the wider debates about educational diversity and equity. In the main, these innovations are "systemic" enough in their own right to be generalisable to other students, *e.g.* those at risk from disadvantaged backgrounds, and those who would benefit from more individualised teaching and learning.

The chapter commences by examining, in Section 2, the concept of a rights-based approach to assisting children with special education needs. Section 3 then provides a cross-national overview of the forms in which countries allocate additional resources for students with disabilities, learning difficulties and disadvantages. This is a difficult area in which to compile comprehensive and internationally comparable indicators, and the discussion draws on the latest results from the OECD's on-going collaboration with national authorities. In Section 4, evidence from a series of case studies and the wider research literature is used to identify key ingredients in making more inclusive approaches to education work. The main conclusions are summarised in Section 5, along with priorities for future work.

2. EQUITY AND INCLUSION

Meeting the educational needs of students is part of the development of equitable provision in an inclusive society where individual rights are recognised and protected. The *United Nations Charter on the Rights of the Child*, for instance, states that all children have a right to education and as a consequence the right to make progress. Failure to provide education and create the conditions for individual progress may be seen as a denial of a child's rights. Such thinking underlies the approaches to individual education planning for students with disabilities based on human rights legislation in the United States, for example. The call by Sen (1992) for efforts to ensure that people have equal access to basic capabilities such as the ability to be healthy, well-fed, housed, integrated into the community, participate in community and public life and enjoy self-respect has similarities to the rights-based approach of the UN Charter. Denial of these rights or capabilities with regard to children can be seen as a precursor of social exclusion (Evans *et al.*, 2002).

There are many discussions in the literature on the concept of equity (see Hutmacher *et al.*, 2001). There are four basic interpretations of equity which can be applied to educational policy and practice. Demeuse *et al.* (2001), based on OECD (1993):

- Equity of access or equality of opportunity: Do all individuals (or groups of individuals) have the same chance of progressing to a particular level in the education system?

- Equity in terms of learning environment or equality of means: Do all individuals enjoy equivalent learning conditions? This question is generally taken to mean: Do disadvantaged individuals or groups benefit from a learning environment equivalent to advantaged individuals or groups in terms of the level of training of their teachers

---

[1]. The work reported in this chapter would not have been possible without support from the United States Department of Education, Office of Special Education and Rehabilitative Services.

and other staff, and the quantity and quality of teaching resources and approaches?

- Equity in production or equality of achievement (or results): Do students all master, with the same degree of expertise, skills or knowledge designated as goals of the education system? Most particularly, do individuals from different backgrounds achieve, over the period of education or training, equivalent outcomes? Do all individuals have the same chance of earning the same qualifications when they leave, and can they do so, independent of their circumstances of origin? This concern about equality in achievement is founded on an ideal of corrective justice (Crahay, 2000) and is inevitably accompanied by a desire to narrow the gap between high and low performers from the start to the end of their programme of education (Bressoux, 1993).

- Equity in using the results of education: Once they have left the education system, do individuals or groups of individuals have the same chances of using their acquired knowledge and skills in employment and wider community life?

Rawls (1971) in his *Theory of Justice* argued that to achieve society's equity goals institutions should be biased in favour of the disadvantaged in terms of resource allocation. Brighouse (2000) takes up this issue from the point of view of disabled students. He points out that for many disabled students no amount of additional resources will assist them to achieve the same level of performance as many non-disabled peers. From this perspective it would clearly be inequitable to give all of an education system's resources to disabled students at the expense of the more able. However, some additional resources are required, *e.g.* signing interpretation for deaf students to help them access the curriculum. Thus, when taking account of the whole population of students, the question is how to decide the extent of the available resources that should be provided for students with disabilities.

From the point of view of thinking of equity as achieving similar outcomes or reducing the variance of performance across the student population, considering students with disabilities presents a similar challenge: the question is what degree of variance in outcomes is acceptable. A rights-based approach can to some extent side-step this issue since from this perspective all children should be making progress and the problem becomes how to assess individual rate of progress across the curriculum in a way which can constructively promote learning, in contrast to a single group-based outcome measure. From this viewpoint variance in rate of progress might be a better indicator of the extent to which educational equity is being achieved.

Countries aim to meet these conditions by providing additional resources to assist students with the most difficulties. This may be seen as an application of positive discrimination under Rawls' model of social justice. His "difference principle" (Rawls, 1971) argued for institutions to be structured with a built-in bias in favour of the disadvantaged. It is now widely accepted that the education of disabled students could not be achieved without additional resources being made available for them if they are to access the curriculum on anything like an equal basis with non-disabled students. Disabled students need additional resources to be able to profit, as other students do, from "the benefits that education provides opportunities for" (Brighouse, 2000).

These arguments suggest that one way to start an investigation of equity for students with various forms of learning difficulty is through analysing the additional resources supplied to meet their needs. This approach has a number of advantages, especially in developing a method open to making valid international comparisons. First, it makes no strong prior assumptions about the national approach used to gather information on students with difficulties, focusing instead on the criterion that additional resources are provided for some categories of students. Thus the approach can include those with disabilities, those with learning difficulties or those with disadvantages. This is important, since countries have developed very different conceptual frameworks applying to such students, and as a consequence they use different models for defining and assessing their needs (see OECD, 2000, 2003). Second, resources and their distribution are important in educational policy making, and drawing together international data on resource allocation can help raise questions about priorities and the effectiveness of different forms of educational provision.

CHAPTER 1

DIVERSITY, INCLUSION AND EQUITY:
INSIGHTS FROM SPECIAL NEEDS PROVISION

> Box 1.1 **Development of international indicators on students with disabilities, learning difficulties and disadvantages**
>
> The data presented in this chapter are part of an on-going collaboration with participating member countries that started in 1996 to develop comparative data on students with disabilities, learning difficulties and disadvantages. The task is made especially complicated because of the different conceptual frameworks and definitions relating to such students that exist across countries. A significant aspect of the collaboration is a continual process of refinement of data quality and quantity, checking and consultation. Countries are using the process to improve their national data collections to fill gaps and ensure greater consistency and clarity in definitions and coverage.
>
> The approach to data collection that is agreed with the countries is to bring together national data sets which apply to students in schools who are receiving additional resources to help them access the curriculum. Data are collected from countries in as disaggregated a form as possible and then grouped into broad categories based on explicit definitions and agreement among the countries. Countries provided the data in a form that removed double-counting if students were in more than one type of programme. Details of the methodology and classifications are provided in OECD (2000, 2003). The full data set is provided on the OECD website so that other researchers can analyse the data and assess the implications of grouping them in different ways.
>
> The data in this chapter focus mainly on the compulsory years of schooling, which is typically from around age 6-16 in most countries. The pre-school, upper secondary and tertiary levels are also very important for students with disabilities, learning difficulties and disadvantages, but generally there are fewer data available for those sectors.
>
> Data are presented for those OECD countries and in the case of Canada, provinces, for which relevant data are available. If a country or province is not mentioned this does not mean that it does not provide additional resources for such students. It simply means that data are not available on the indicators concerned in an internationally comparable form. The data focus on 1999 and are the most recently available that have been through the verification process. They are a selection from a much more extensive set of information which is available in OECD (2003). More recent developments in national programmes and classification systems will be progressively verified for international comparative purposes and included in future OECD publications.

3. INTERNATIONAL DATA ON SPECIAL NEEDS PROVISION

The OECD has been working with national authorities since 1996 to develop internationally comparable data on students with disabilities, learning difficulties and disadvantages. A full account of the methodology and results is provided in OECD (2000, 2003). Box 1.1 summarises the processes involved and the current status of the work. In broad terms, countries have been asked to provide data on all students for whom additional resources are made available. The data have been disaggregated into three cross-national categories covering students with defined disabilities, difficulties and disadvantages.[2] These are referred to as cross-national categories "A", "B" and "C", respectively. National representatives made this disaggregation, and the results were discussed and agreed at international meetings.

---

2. The Appendix to this chapter summarises the allocation of national categories to the three cross-national categories A, B, and C and provides their definitions as they appear in the Instruction Manual for data gathering and classification. OECD (2000) and OECD (2003) provide further details of the differences among the categories.

Education Policy Analysis © OECD 2003

One outcome of this procedure is summarised in the Appendix, which classifies the programmes through which countries indicated they provide additional resources for specified groups of students. The Appendix provides some indication of the complexity of the task. The number of categories used varies widely from country to country, as do their national labels. The Appendix also shows the classification of students in receipt of additional resources in the three broad cross-national categories of disabilities, difficulties and disadvantages. Those in the "disabilities" category have clear organic bases for their difficulties. Those in the "difficulties" category have learning and behaviour difficulties which do not appear to be due to either a clear organic basis or social disadvantage. Those in the "disadvantages" category receive additional educational resources due to aspects of their social and/or language background.

Countries also provided information on the place of education for those in receipt of additional resources (special schools, special classes in regular schools, and regular classes), the gender composition of students, and aspects of schools and staffing. In addition they provided some qualitative material on legal frameworks and facilitators and barriers to inclusion and equity. In all, a very extensive set of information has been compiled to date, and only some of the indicators are presented in this chapter.

3.1 Students with disabilities

Figure 1.1 shows the variation in the proportion of students receiving additional resources for disabilities in compulsory education (cross-national category A). Among the 16 countries concerned the proportion ranges from 0.6% in Mexico to 4.6% in the United States. The median value is 2.1%, and the inter-quartile range is from 1.6% to 3.1%.

These differences in proportions are not easy to interpret. As can be seen from the Appendix, countries differ substantially in both the number and type of programmes included in the disabilities category. Since it is unlikely that the "organic" bases of disability differ greatly among countries, it seems most likely that the different proportions in Figure 1.1 reflect national differences in the conceptualisation of disability, identification

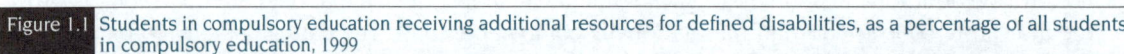
Figure 1.1 Students in compulsory education receiving additional resources for defined disabilities, as a percentage of all students in compulsory education, 1999

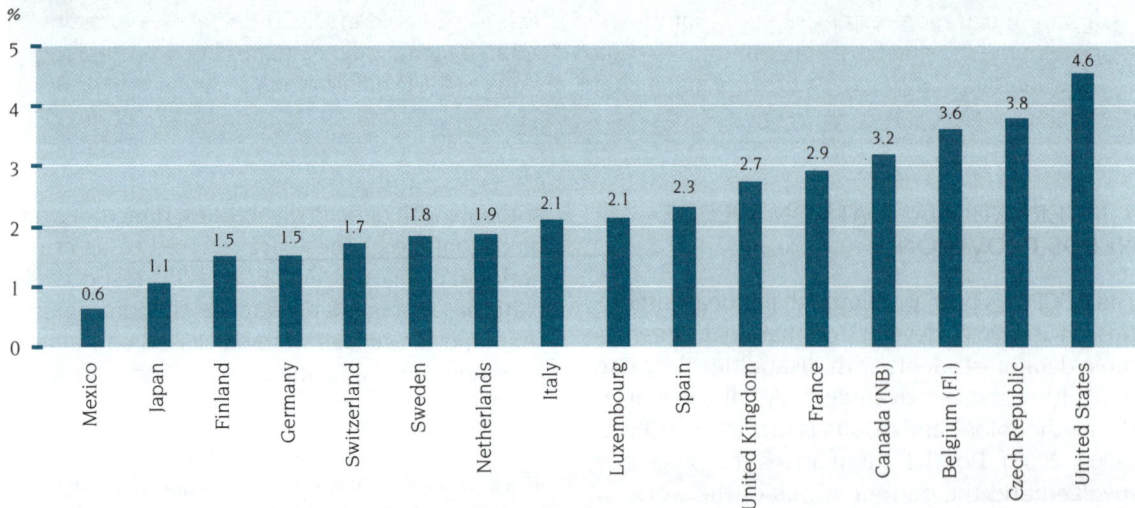

Note: For France, students in Ministry of Health programmes have been added to the data provided by the Ministry of Education. This probably slightly inflates the percentage for France relative to other countries that did not provide data on students with disabilities outside the education system.
Source: Based on the classifications (category A) in the Appendix. For further details see OECD (2003).

CHAPTER 1

DIVERSITY, INCLUSION AND EQUITY:
INSIGHTS FROM SPECIAL NEEDS PROVISION

procedures, educational practices, comprehensiveness of provision, and policy priorities. Such variation suggests that there are differences between countries in the ways in which they try to overcome the effects of disabilities, and this could in principle have an impact on the outcomes for different types of students.

Figure 1.2 shows where students with disabilities who are in receipt of additional resources are being educated – special schools, special classes in regular schools, or regular classes. What is immediately clear is that some countries, *e.g.* Spain, the United States, Italy and Canada (New Brunswick) make extensive use of regular classes while others prefer to use special schools, *e.g.* Belgium (Flemish Community), the Czech Republic, Germany and the Netherlands. Some countries make extensive use of special classes in regular schools, *e.g.* France, Finland and Japan.

There is not a clear statistical relationship between proportions identified in Figure 1.1, and the use of one or other of the school locations recorded in Figure 1.2. For example, it could be expected that countries with a relatively high proportion of students in the disabilities category may make relatively extensive use of regular classes since presumably the programmes of such countries would encompass more students with relatively "mild" disabilities. However, the data indicate that this is not the case. Differences will certainly reflect different national policies concerning inclusion, which may in themselves be influenced by features of regular schools and their curriculum, and the training and attitudes of teachers which may facilitate or obstruct inclusion. In addition, there may be features of special schools which are viewed by parents and educators as desirable. It is clear, however, that the same type of disabled students may be included in regular classes in

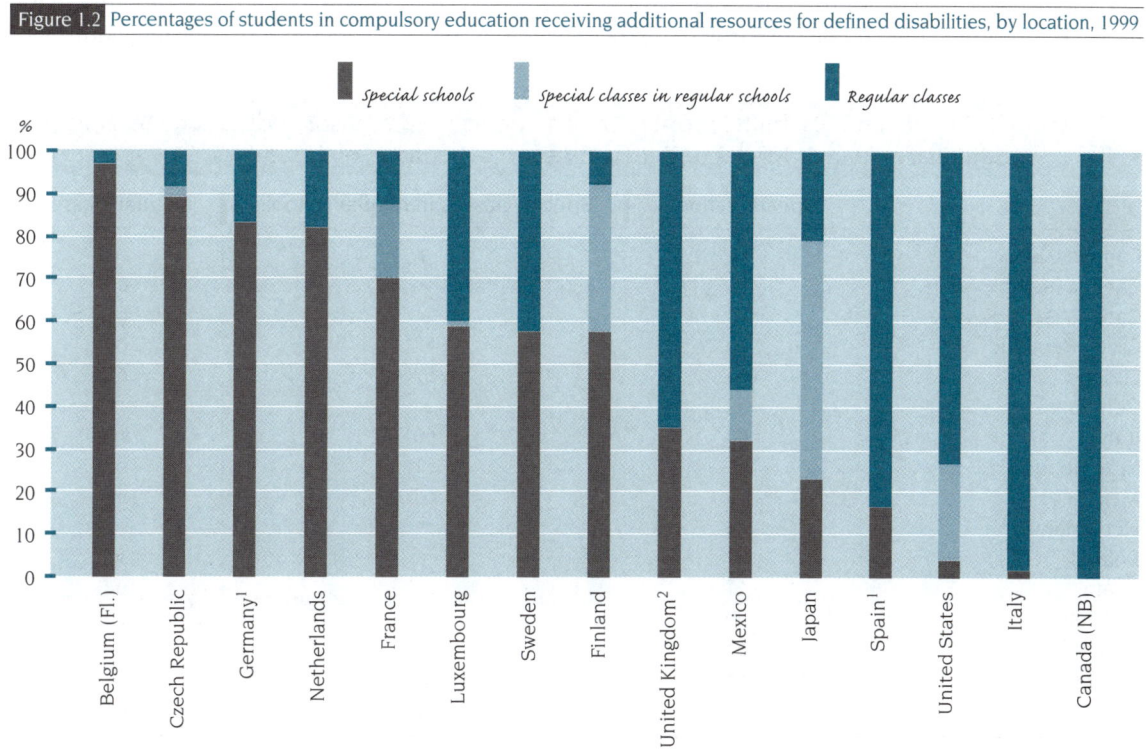

Figure 1.2 Percentages of students in compulsory education receiving additional resources for defined disabilities, by location, 1999

1. Students in special classes are included in special schools.
2. Students in special classes are included in regular classes.
Source: Based on the classifications (category A) in the Appendix. For further details see OECD (2003).
Data for Figure 1.2, p. 35.

one country, but in a special school in another. The substantial differences between countries in both the proportion of students who receive additional resources, and the location of their education, raise questions about potentially differential impacts on outcomes for individual students.

Gender differences among students with disabilities

Gender differences are especially notable for students with disabilities, as Table 1.1 shows. For almost all countries there is a male to female ratio of about 60 to 40. As is discussed later when data on age are presented, the preponderance of males among students classified as having disabilities is evident at all ages, and if anything the proportion of males tends to rise with age (*e.g.* in the Netherlands).

In all the countries for which data in cross-national category A are available, there are more males than females in programmes providing additional resources for defined disabilities, and more boys find themselves in some form of special provision (special schools, special classes or with extra help in regular classes) than do girls. Some of the possible reasons for these gender differences are discussed later in the chapter.

3.2 Students with learning difficulties

Figure 1.3 shows the number of students receiving additional resources within the period of compulsory education who are considered to fall into the "difficulties" category for countries able to supply data (cross-national category B). Those countries that have no national categories falling into this classification are included in the chart and entered as a "zero". The median proportion of students in the defined difficulties category is 2.3% and the inter-quartile range from 0.3% to 7.5% shows an amount of variability far in excess of that found in the corresponding data for students in the disabilities category (1.6% to 3.1%). If the analysis is limited to those countries with programmes in the difficulties category, data are available from 12 countries. They provide a median percentage of 5.9% and inter-quartile range from 1.8% to 8.8%. Several countries have particularly high proportions of students receiving additional

Table 1.1 **Gender and disability: proportion of students in compulsory education receiving additional resources for defined disabilities who are male, by location, 1999 (%)**

	Special schools	Special classes in regular schools	Regular classes
Canada (Alberta)	a	a	61
Canada (New Brunswick)	a	a	66
Canada (Saskatchewan)	a	a	61
Czech Republic	60	52	60
Finland	65	67	66
Germany	62	x	m
Italy	63	60	m
Luxembourg	61	87	65
Mexico	59	63	61
Netherlands	68	m	m
Poland	53	m	m
Spain	61	x	62
Sweden	59	m	56
Switzerland	65	a	a
Turkey	65	62	m
United Kingdom	68	x	68

a: Data not applicable because the category does not apply.
m: Data not available.
x: Data included in another column: in Germany and Spain the data are included in the special schools column; in the United Kingdom the data are included in the regular classes column.

Source: Based on the classifications (category A) in the Appendix. For further details see OECD (2003).

CHAPTER 1

DIVERSITY, INCLUSION AND EQUITY: INSIGHTS FROM SPECIAL NEEDS PROVISION

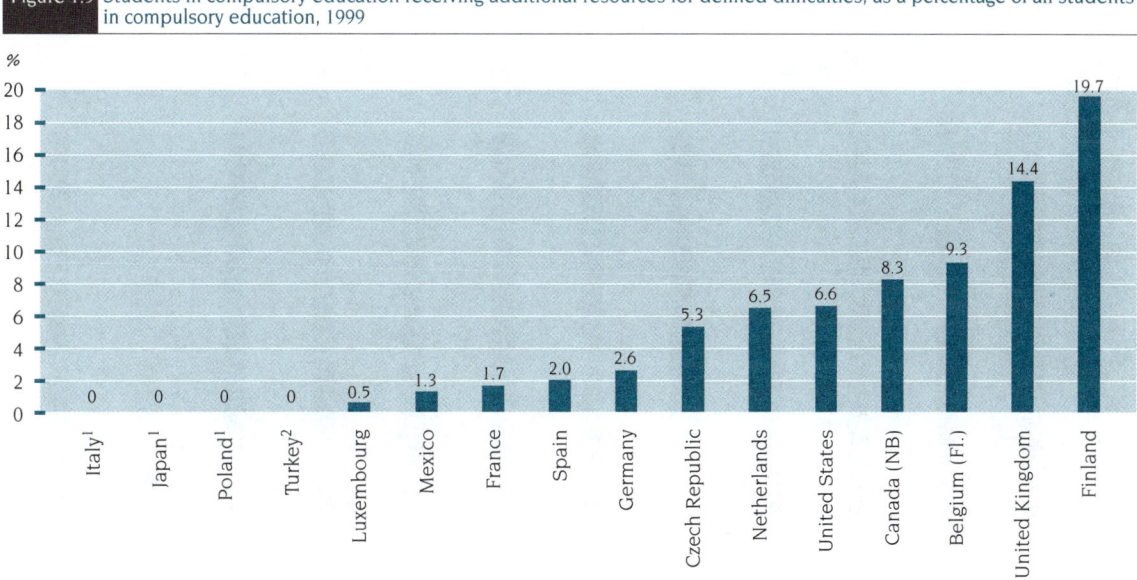

Figure 1.3 Students in compulsory education receiving additional resources for defined difficulties, as a percentage of all students in compulsory education, 1999

1. No national categories falling within the cross-national category of defined difficulties.
2. In Turkey, the only national category falling within the cross-national category of defined difficulties is "Gifted and talented", which has been excluded from the analysis.
Source: Based on the classifications (category B) in the Appendix. For further details see OECD (2003).

resources for defined learning difficulties: Canada (New Brunswick) (8.3%), Belgium (Flemish Community) (9.3%), the United Kingdom (14.4%), and Finland (19.7%). In general, it appears that when such categories are recognised in national systems the numbers of students receiving additional resources are considerable.

Compared with disabled students, those with defined learning difficulties are much more likely to receive their education in regular schools. Figure 1.4 shows the distribution of students by location for 12 countries which could provide the data. In Germany the majority of these students are in special schools, and all are in special classes in France. The Netherlands uses these two forms of provision more or less equally. In the other countries regular school provision is the most common pattern, and although there may be use of special classes in regular schools, the data often do not allow this breakdown to be made.

Gender differences among students with learning difficulties

Table 1.2 gives gender ratios for students with defined difficulties (cross-national category B) classified by location of programme. As was the case for students with disabilities, there are more males in such programmes than females: the percentage of males is typically between 60% and 70%.

3.3 Students with disadvantages

Figure 1.5 shows the proportion of students receiving additional resources within compulsory education who are considered to fall within the "disadvantages" classification (cross-national category C) for different countries. Countries with no students included in this category are entered as a zero. The median for category C students as a percentage of all students in compulsory education is 0.3%. The inter-quartile range is from zero to 4.5%. This median percentage is substantially lower than that for students with disabilities and difficulties (2.1% and 2.3% respectively). Limiting the analysis to those nine countries with data on programmes providing additional resources falling within cross-national category C, the median percentage is 1.0% and the inter-quartile range is from 0.2% to 8.7%. These figures, with particularly high values for France (11.1%) and the Netherlands (16.5%), indicate that when categories of students with defined disadvantages are included in national systems the numbers of students receiving additional resources are considerable.

Education Policy Analysis © OECD 2003

CHAPTER 1

DIVERSITY, INCLUSION AND EQUITY:
INSIGHTS FROM SPECIAL NEEDS PROVISION

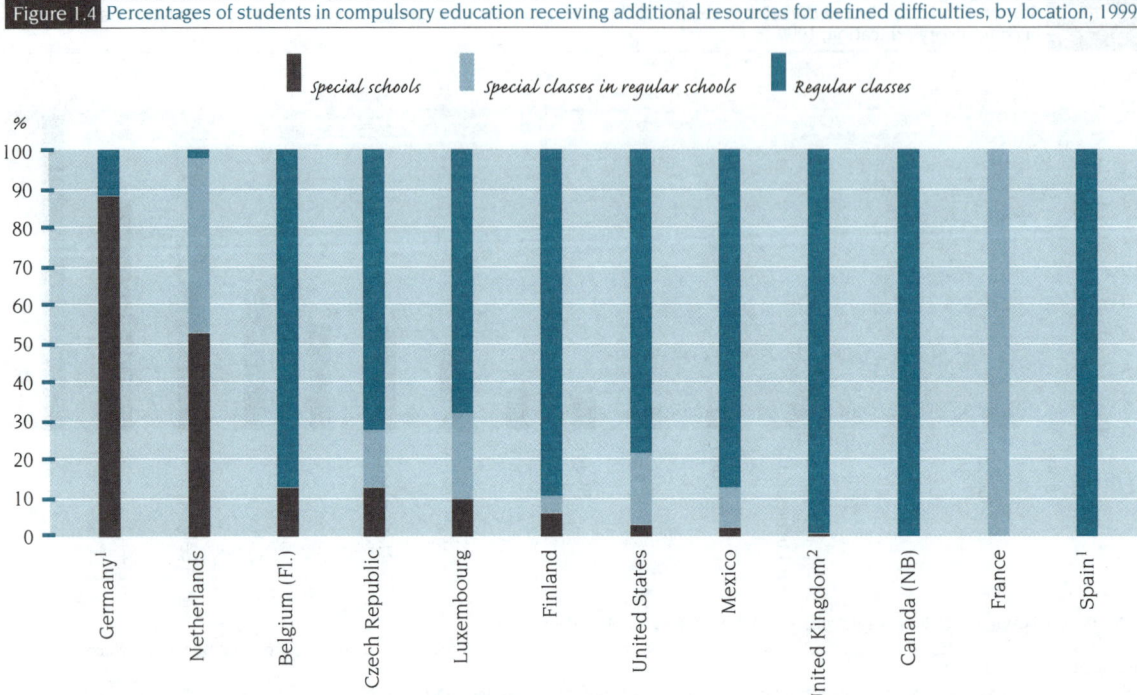

Figure 1.4 Percentages of students in compulsory education receiving additional resources for defined difficulties, by location, 1999

1. Students in special classes are included in special schools.
2. Students in special classes are included in regular classes.
Source: Based on the classifications (category B) in the Appendix. For further details see OECD (2003).
Data for Figure 1.4, p. 35.

Table 1.2 Gender and learning difficulties: proportion of students in compulsory education receiving additional resources for defined difficulties who are male, by location, 1999 (%)

	Special schools	Special classes in regular schools	Regular classes
Belgium (Flemish Community)	69	m	m
Canada (Alberta)	a	a	67
Canada (New Brunswick)	a	a	69
Czech Republic	57	66	74
Finland	66	76	65
France	m	59	m
Germany	64	x	m
Luxembourg	66	55	60
Mexico	67	62	60
Netherlands	68	59	m
Spain	m	x	59
Switzerland	m	62	m
United Kingdom	68	x	69

a: Data not applicable because the category does not apply.
m: Data not available.
x: Data included in another column: in Germany and Spain the data are included in the special schools column; in the United Kingdom the data are included in the regular classes column.

Source: Based on the classifications (category B) in the Appendix. For further details see OECD (2003).

18 © OECD 2003 *Education Policy Analysis*

CHAPTER 1

DIVERSITY, INCLUSION AND EQUITY:
INSIGHTS FROM SPECIAL NEEDS PROVISION

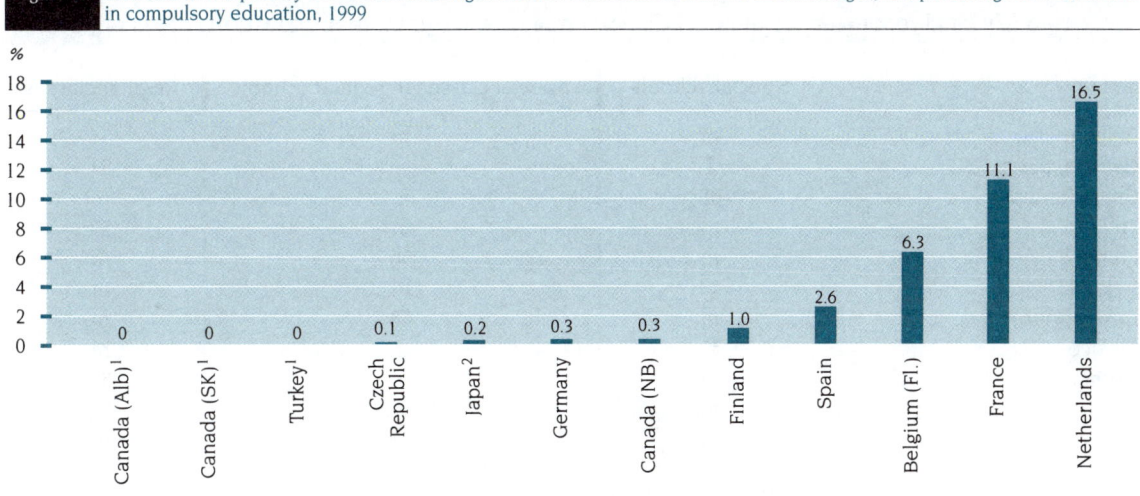

Figure 1.5 Students in compulsory education receiving additional resources for defined disadvantages, as a percentage of all students in compulsory education, 1999

1. No national categories falling within the cross-national category of defined disadvantages.
2. The data from Japan refer to students in public schools only.
Source: Based on the classifications (category C) in the Appendix. For further details see OECD (2003).

Figure 1.6 shows the locations of students receiving additional resources for defined disadvantages for the eight countries who supplied this data. The majority of countries educate all of these students in regular classes. The Czech Republic uses exclusively special schools. Belgium (Flemish Community) and France make some use of special classes in regular schools, although the large majority of students with defined disadvantages in these two countries are in regular classes.

Gender differences among students with disadvantages

Table 1.3 gives gender ratios for students in receipt of additional resources for defined disadvantages (cross-national category C) in compulsory schooling. The gender ratios are provided separately for different types of location where such distinctions apply and the data are available. For all of the countries concerned there are more males than females in such programmes. The proportion of

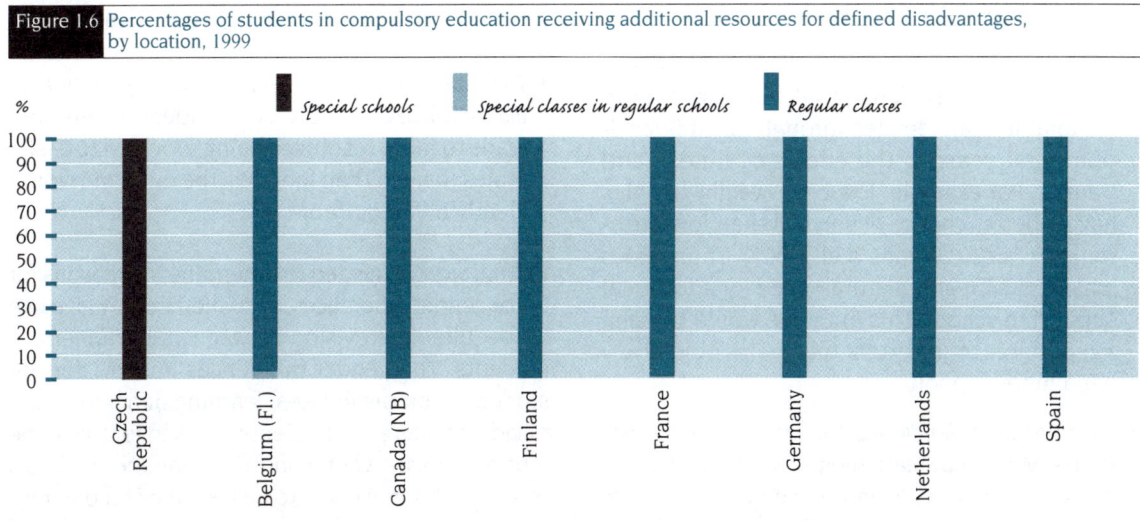

Figure 1.6 Percentages of students in compulsory education receiving additional resources for defined disadvantages, by location, 1999

Source: Based on the classifications (category C) in the Appendix. For further details see OECD (2003).
Data for Figure 1.6, p. 35.

Education Policy Analysis © OECD 2003

CHAPTER 1

DIVERSITY, INCLUSION AND EQUITY:
INSIGHTS FROM SPECIAL NEEDS PROVISION

Table 1.3 **Gender and disadvantages: proportion of students in compulsory education receiving additional resources for defined disadvantages who are male, by location, 1999 (%)**

	Special schools	Special classes in regular schools	Regular classes
Belgium (Flemish Community)	m	m	51
Canada (New Brunswick)	a	a	57
Czech Republic	68	m	m
Finland	m	m	53
France	m	56	m
Ireland	53	m	m
Luxembourg	m	58	m
Mexico	52	x	m
Netherlands	m	m	51
Spain	m	x	55
Switzerland	m	51	m

a: Data not applicable because the category does not apply.
m: Data not available.
x: Data included in another column: in Mexico and Spain the data are included in the special schools column.
Source: Based on the classifications (category C) in the Appendix. For further details see OECD (2003).

males is typically between 50% and 60%, but this is a more even distribution than for students with disabilities (Table 1.1) and learning difficulties (Table 1.2) where the proportion of males was often at least 60%.

The data show that for all three cross-national categories, the proportion of males generally exceeds the proportion of females by a ratio of about 3 to 2. The proportion of males is particularly high in the group with defined difficulties (category B). A number of possible reasons can be identified, and each may play some role:

- *Male children are more prone to illness and trauma*. There is some evidence that males are more vulnerable than females throughout the developmental years to the effects of illness and trauma. For example, low birth-weight females have a better chance of survival than low birth-weight males (Lemons *et al.*, 2001). Thus males may have a greater "natural" need for additional support in school. This outcome would be seen as equitable to the extent that males objectively need more support.

- *Males externalize their "feelings" in school more openly than females*. Males may make themselves more likely to be noticed in schools and consequently labeled. Recent examples of extreme violence perpetrated by males in schools highlights the point.

- *Schooling is becoming increasingly "feminised"*. The greater proportion of female teachers in schools, especially during the primary years, has been well documented (OECD, 2001b). Also the increased emphasis in some countries on the need for academic learning rather than practical skills may be moving schooling away from traditional types of male activity. The net result may be that males are having more difficulties in school; the fact, noted earlier, that the "difficulties" category generally has a higher proportion of males than do the disabilities and disadvantages categories may reflect these issues.

- *The education of males is given greater priority than that of females*. If this view is indeed taken, and leads to more resources being provided to assist males in need than females, the outcome would clearly be inequitable.

Further work is needed to determine the reasons for these gender differences, and whether they give rise to inequitable provision between male and female students. The gender differences in provision for students with disabilities, learning difficulties and disadvantages are sufficiently marked for this to be a priority focus when countries examine the basis by which children come to be identified for different programmes, and the long-term consequences of participation in those programmes.

CHAPTER 1

DIVERSITY, INCLUSION AND EQUITY:
INSIGHTS FROM SPECIAL NEEDS PROVISION

Table 1.4 **The number and size of special schools in compulsory education**

	Number of special schools per 100 000 students enrolled in compulsory education	Size of special schools (average number of students enrolled)
Belgium (Flemish Community)	37	132
Canada (New Brunswick)	0	0
Czech Republic	58	70
Finland	45	45
France	22	65
Germany	29	121
Italy	1	26
Mexico	82	12
Netherlands	50	99
Poland	15	71
Spain[1]	11	35
Sweden	62	17
Switzerland	46	37
Turkey	2	68
United Kingdom	16	64

1. The data for Spain refer to all levels of school.
Source: OECD (2003).

3.4 Provision in special schools

It was seen earlier that countries differ markedly in the extent to which students with disabilities are located in special schools (see Figure 1.2). Table 1.4 provides another perspective on this issue by documenting the number of special schools per 100 000 students enrolled in compulsory education. It confirms the results of the data on location of education as presented in the previous figures. Canada (New Brunswick) has no special schools at this level, and in Italy there are only very few special schools. On the other hand, in the Czech Republic, Mexico and Sweden there are a relatively large numbers of special schools: 58, 82 and 62 per 100 000 students in compulsory education, respectively.

To avoid providing a misleading picture the size of these schools must be taken into account. For instance, as Table 1.4 shows, Sweden has a relatively large number (62 per 100 000 students) of rather small special schools (17 students on average). This contrasts to France with relatively few (22 per 100 000 students) but comparatively large special schools (65 students, on average). Two countries with relatively large special schools, Germany (121 students on average) and the Netherlands (99 students), also happen to be the two countries where special schools include a large proportion of students with learning difficulties. These are further examples of where the marked differences among countries can help to raise questions about the basis of special needs provision, and the substantial variations provide scope for the effects of different approaches to be evaluated.

Figure 1.7 shows data from 15 countries on the age distribution of students enrolled in special schools. In general, only about 1% of 5-6 year-olds are in special schools in most countries, and the proportion starts to rise from around 8 years of age before reaching a plateau around the ages 12-15 and then declining rapidly. These increases in the proportion of students in special schools, which are quite substantial (in Germany it increases six-fold between the ages 6 and 15) presumably reflect the movement of students out of regular schools and special classes into special schools. The decline beyond around age 15 most likely reflects the fact that most such students do not continue with their education beyond the compulsory years, a conclusion generally supported from the inspection of data on individual categories of disabilities (OECD, 2003).

There are some notable exceptions to the general pattern in Figure 1.7. Japan shows a flat gradient

Education Policy Analysis © OECD 2003

CHAPTER 1

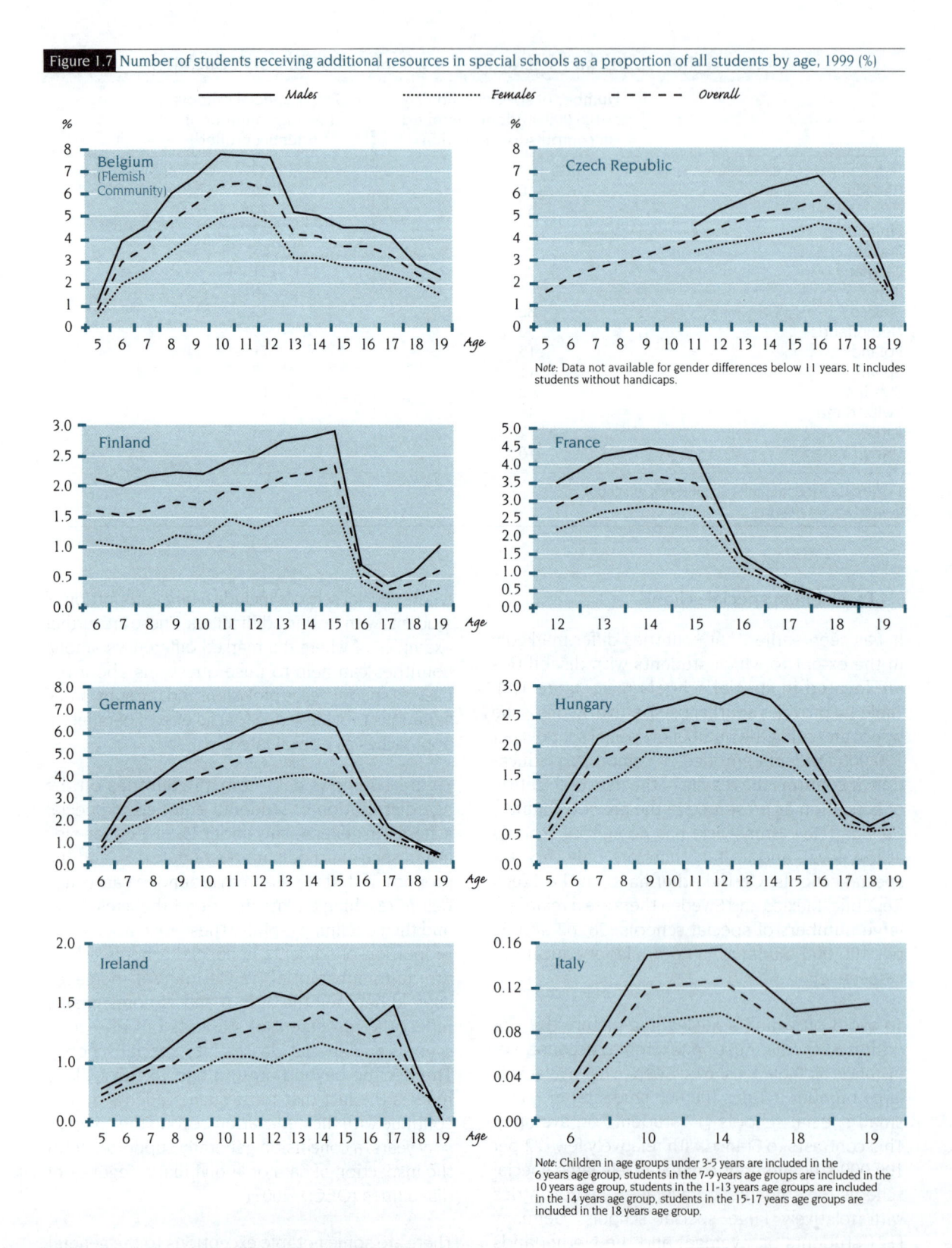

DIVERSITY, INCLUSION AND EQUITY:
INSIGHTS FROM SPECIAL NEEDS PROVISION

Figure 1.7 Number of students receiving additional resources in special schools as a proportion of all students by age, 1999 (%)

——— Males   ·········· Females   - - - - - Overall

Note: Data not available for gender differences below 11 years. It includes students without handicaps.

Note: Children in age groups under 3-5 years are included in the 6 years age group, students in the 7-9 years age groups are included in the 10 years age group, students in the 11-13 years age groups are included in the 14 years age group, students in the 15-17 years age groups are included in the 18 years age group.

Note: The scale on the vertical axis differs from country to country.
Source: Data have been supplied by the Ministries of Education.

CHAPTER 1

DIVERSITY, INCLUSION AND EQUITY:
INSIGHTS FROM SPECIAL NEEDS PROVISION

Figure 1.7 (continued) Number of students receiving additional resources in special schools as a proportion of all students by age, 1999 (%)

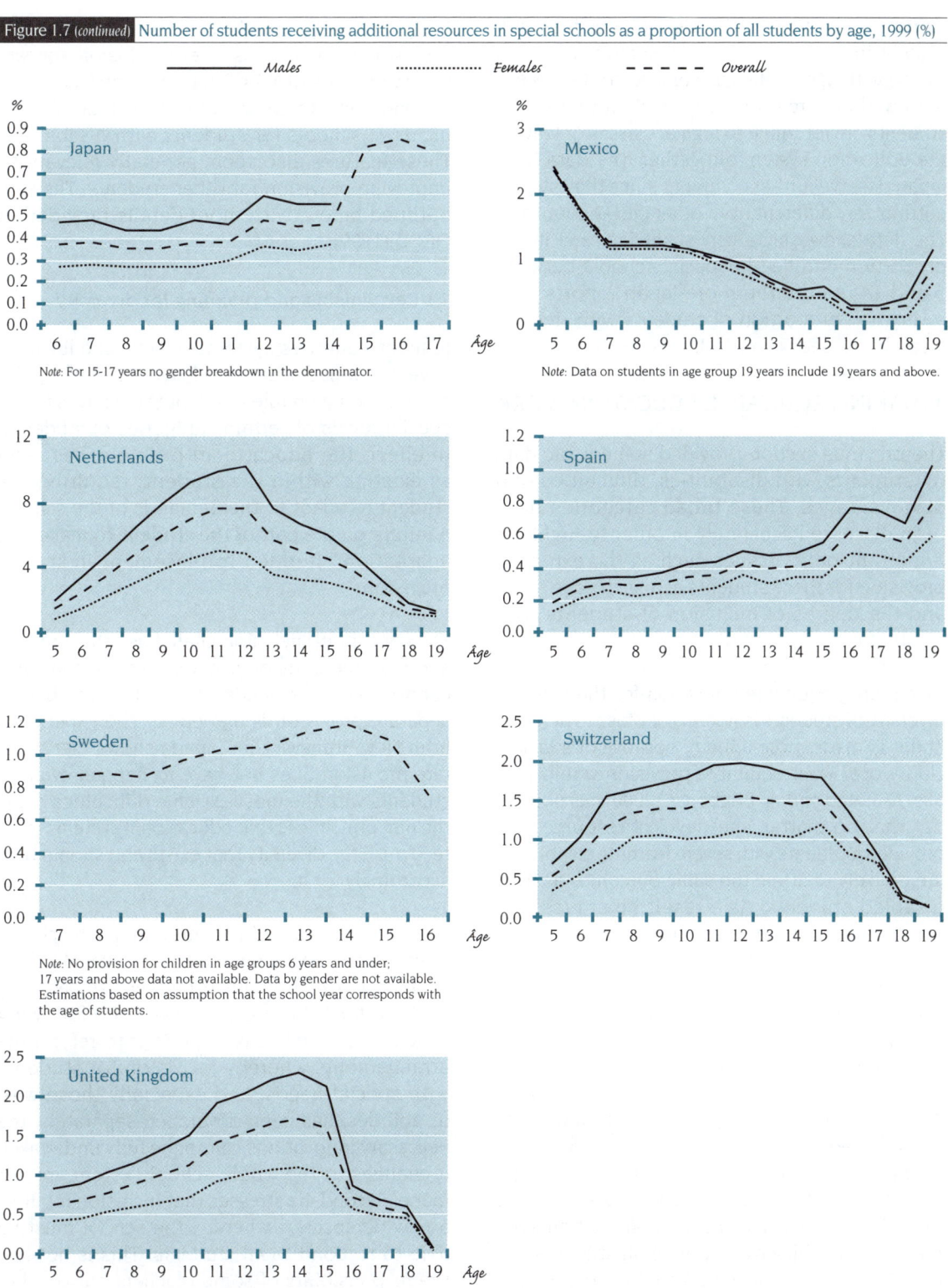

Note: For 15-17 years no gender breakdown in the denominator.

Note: Data on students in age group 19 years include 19 years and above.

Note: No provision for children in age groups 6 years and under; 17 years and above data not available. Data by gender are not available. Estimations based on assumption that the school year corresponds with the age of students.

Note: The scale on the vertical axis differs from country to country.
Source: Data have been supplied by the Ministries of Education.
Data for Figure 1.7, p. 36.

Education Policy Analysis © OECD 2003

rising quickly at age 14-15. Mexico's declines with a slight increase at age 18 and Spain's continues to rise with age. In the case of Mexico the declining numbers are difficult to explain unless the students are returning to regular classes or leaving the education system altogether. The data from Japan deserve further comment since they show a pattern very different from other OECD countries. The data show only a very slight increase in the proportion enrolled in special schools between 6 and 14, and furthermore Japan reports only a very low proportion of students with defined disabilities (see Figure 1.1).

4. MAKING EQUITABLE EDUCATION WORK

The previous section provided some basic data on students with disabilities, difficulties and disadvantages. These broad categories have been discussed separately in order to highlight important policy issues such as the extent of provision for these students across the age range and the degree of inclusion of students with disabilities.

Developing equitable education for the growing diversity of students is not an easy task to achieve, and it is made more difficult because of a lack of clarity over what equitable provision would look like. As noted earlier, Brighouse (2000) has pointed out that no matter what level of resources are provided, students with severe learning disabilities are unlikely to attain the same outcomes as non-disabled students. As a result he argues that equity, conceived of as the attainment of equal outcomes for all students is flawed. Thus, a simple measure of reduction in inequality in performance cannot be considered an adequate indicator of equity. What is needed is a focus on the degree of inequality that is acceptable.

At this stage possibly the best way forward is to consider equity as a process, and in doing so to make sure that full consideration is given to providing additional resources for those who need them during the period of education. Cost-effective methods of achieving equity for all students still need to be fully evaluated. What follows provides some indication of the kinds of ingredients that need to be in place to meet the needs of the most challenging students.

Following visits to eight countries and intensive case studies of schools where inclusion appears to be working well, OECD has identified a number of conditions which are important in developing inclusive schools for students with disabilities. These features also seem generally relevant to improving provision for other students. They are outlined below, with more details provided in OECD (1999).

4.1 Recognising and planning for diversity

In many countries systems of special education have developed separately in a context of regular schools being unable to adapt themselves to the special needs of certain categories of students. In effect, the educational problem was seen as existing within the student, requiring the student to adapt to the demands of the school. A failure on the part of the student to make this adaptation often led to placement in special provision.

The concept of inclusion challenges this practice and puts the onus on schools to show that they cannot meet the needs of the students before separate provision is agreed to. The experience from New Brunswick in Canada shows that separate provision does not have to happen even for students with the most extreme difficulties. Thus the first principle is that educational systems must recognise the diversity that exists and should plan accordingly for it.

Following 10 years of reform of Spanish schools intended to make them more inclusive, Marchesi (1997) speaking from his experience as Secretary of State for Education, came to the following conclusions. First, it is important to reform the arrangements whereby provision for students with special needs, and especially those with disabilities, has been developed separately; the necessary innovations cannot be fully undertaken if changes to the whole school system are not made. Second, he stresses that inclusion requires a new perspective whereby the school must be able to respond to all students. This is not just the responsibility of some teachers but of all of them working in the context of the school as a whole, which requires rethinking of the school's educational aims, organisation, teaching and assessment methods to properly provide for all students. Third, the education system must be sensitive to changes in society and be able to adapt to them as quickly as possible in new and evolving economic and social environments which include the greater presence of different cultures, increases in racist and xenophobic movements, and changes in family structure and social organisation.

4.2 Using accountability and evaluation for improvement

Accountability is a policy issue of great importance which can be furthered by school inspection systems or the comparison of examination results based on nationally (or internationally) standardised tests of academic achievement. These practices can however work against inclusion if for instance they do not take account of students' abilities at school entry. Accountability mechanisms need to focus on the difference that schools and teachers are making, and not just absolute measures of student outcomes. A "value added" perspective on accountability and evaluation can also help justify additional resources in the context of inclusion. In Italy, for instance, inclusion is predicated on smaller class sizes and smaller class sizes are associated with improved performance for students with disadvantages. The benefits of smaller classes for disadvantaged students have also been shown in the United States (Nye, 2001).

Accountability procedures may also have the incidental effects of discouraging schools from taking on children who are likely to perform poorly in examinations, of encouraging schools to expel children they find difficult to teach, or of tempting schools to omit children with learning difficulties from testing programmes. Thurlow (1997) refers to some two-thirds of students with disabilities in schools in the United States as having been excluded from the 1992 administration of the National Assessment of Educational Progress (US Federal Law now requires their inclusion). Other countries also point out that flexibility in the examination process is important for inclusion and schools should be willing to keep disabled students in school beyond the normal school leaving age if this is requested.

4.3 Professional development of staff

The professional development of teachers and other staff through pre-service and in-service training is a key issue in the development of inclusive schooling systems. A survey of training programmes in OECD countries (Magrab, 1999) identified this area as high priority, an immense challenge and in need of considerable extension. Teachers must develop what Marchesi (1997) describes as interest and competence in inclusion. By interest he means teachers' attitudes, their theories about the education of students with disabilities, difficulties and disadvantages, and their willingness to contribute to their education. Inclusive attitudes should certainly be formed during initial training, and renewed and extended throughout teachers' careers. By competence he is of course referring to their skills. Based on discussions in the eight countries visited, the following practices are particularly important for making inclusive education effective: working as the special education co-ordinator; team teaching; developing mutual support between teachers; effective collaboration through discussion and a problem-solving approach; the pedagogy of curriculum differentiation; the development of individual education programmes; and the monitoring of progress.

Developing the skills required for such practices were prominent features of the training programmes in Canada (New Brunswick) and Italy. In Canada (New Brunswick), for example, all initial teacher training courses included assignments designed to introduce trainee teachers to working with children with disabilities. Once appointed to a school, regular class teachers had on-going access to further in-service training for working with students with disabilities, difficulties and disadvantages. In addition to the training of teachers, the co-ordinated development of other professionals to work in inclusive settings is also required (Magrab, 1999).

4.4 External support services

In all the countries visited, schools received substantial additional support for their work with students with disabilities. There are a wide range of professionals identified by countries who serve in support roles. These include: peripatetic teachers with a wide range of specialisations, special needs co-ordinators, teacher assistants and aides, school counsellors, educational psychologists, clinical psychologists, youth service psychologists, psychotherapists, social workers, physiotherapists, speech therapists, occupational therapists, and doctors and nurses. Parents and voluntary bodies are also often closely involved in supportive roles. In Germany and Sweden, young people can meet their national service obligations by working in special needs settings rather than in the armed forces.

Important roles are also played by local education authority advisers and officers who work with schools specifically in the field of special education. These services provide front-line support for students and teachers and are also closely involved in the formal assessment arrangements that all countries undertake in order to allot additional resources to, and make special arrangements for, students with special needs.

In using these additional services to develop effective inclusive provision it is important to consider how they work with the school. One possibility is that they work with the students themselves on a one-to-one basis isolated from the school as a whole. Another is that they support schools and staff efforts to developing effective approaches to teaching disabled students in the school. This latter approach was strongly preferred and the schools visited were working in this way usually having identified a teacher or teachers to co-ordinate support for special needs students in the school. Nevertheless, there were still large differences between the schools in the approach taken by external support services, particularly in the degree to which they explicitly saw themselves as encouraging and supporting schools to solve their own problems. This can be dramatically illustrated by referring to the three districts visited in Iceland. In the first the ratio of special needs students to external support staff was 47:1, in the second 520:1 and in the third 1 320:1. In the last two districts there had been substantial investment in within-school support thus changing the form of the external support. One school indicated that relying on external experts to sort out problems can often involve inordinate delays and inconsequential advice: "if a school can handle the sparks the fire brigade is not required".

4.5 Within-school support services

The extent to which class teachers are able to provide support for special needs students depends not only on their own skills and experience but also on the way in which the organisation of the school helps them to become familiar with the students' needs. In Germany and Italy, for instance, classes containing students with disabilities were smaller than those without such students. In Denmark and Iceland, class teachers stay with the same children during the children's year by year moves up the school. Training given to individual teachers to support particular needs can then be used efficiently across a number of school years.

In effective examples of inclusive practices class teachers and their assistants have access to a network of support provided within the school by teachers with advanced qualifications and associated expertise in special education. In the United Kingdom, special education co-ordinators have the task of co-ordinating the school's work in supporting special needs students. They may assist class teachers in setting individual targets within the context of flexible lesson plans and help in assessing progress. These specialist teachers may also adapt curriculum materials designed to help successive cohorts of children with learning difficulties at particular stages of the syllabus in particular subjects. In addition they from time to time withdraw children for individual work or to cope with crises.

At their best, these special education specialists were fully integrated into the school as a whole, both sharing in the teaching and being members of the school's management team. Their contributions to school management could be as problem-solvers, not just with respect to special education, but in regard to problems generally. They might also have some expertise in aspects of school life affecting all students, for example in assessment of students' progress or in staff appraisal. Where these roles were developed fully, the posts of special education specialists were highly regarded, much sought after, and recognised as stepping stones to school leadership positions.

4.6 Co-operation between schools

Co-operation between schools is often a feature of good practice in inclusive schooling. In developing inclusive practices, the skills of special school teachers are frequently used to support and train teachers in regular schools through outreach practices. The smooth transition of students between the various phases of schooling is also viewed as important. Schools can help children by assuring a free flow of information about those who are moving from one stage of education to the next. Some systems have the flexibility to allow teachers to cross the primary/secondary boundary and carry on giving support to disabled children in the new setting. In one of the German case study schools, for example, primary teachers follow their students for short periods into the comprehensive secondary school in order to help them settle into their new environment.

4.7 Parent and community involvement

The involvement of parents in the successful education of students with disabilities is well documented in the literature (*e.g.* Mittler, 1993). Parents may be involved in schools at many different levels. In Canada (New Brunswick) for instance, they are strongly represented in the school governance process and can influence school policy.

But parents may also have a more direct role. They are often closely involved in the decision making concerning assessment arrangements and in Denmark they can effectively prevent certification of their child as in need of special education. Elsewhere they can support children in classroom work in areas like reading and mathematics. However, in other countries, parents may have relatively little involvement.

Community involvement also seems to be an important feature of effective inclusion, although its incidence varies greatly across countries. In Colorado, in the United States, accountability committees ensure community involvement in the development and evaluation of school improvement. An on-line database forms part of the work of PEAK (Parent Education and Assistance for Kids) the local branch of which also publishes Colorado-based resources for parents and educators wanting to promote inclusion. In Colorado, too, Americacorps volunteers were working in the classroom with children at risk. In Italy, in Rome, professionals and parents and other members of the community work with churches and other voluntary agencies in local provision.

The benefits of wider community involvement are also seen in professional development programmes. In Colorado again, education department, university and parent body representatives had collaborated to implement a project providing in-service training for school leadership teams in developing strategies for inclusive education. In this endeavour they catered for ethnic, cultural and intellectual diversity.

4.8 School organisation and management – opportunities for whole school development

Educating students with disabilities is an issue for the whole school, not just for individual teachers. Furthermore, planning successful inclusion has to go beyond the teaching of traditional subjects and to give close attention to the social and affective side of development.

For example, under the whole school approach in the United Kingdom, head teachers and the school management have to be committed to innovations especially as they are accountable for how the school works, its ethos and in motivating teachers to work for all the children on the roll. In one case study school the head of the upper secondary school and the chairman of the Board of Governors both had experience and strong interest in education for special needs students. Coherence of practices and pastoral care[3] were of particular interest. They had implemented an "assertive discipline" programme across the school adhered to by all teachers. When students transgressed the rules of acceptable behaviour there were constructive punishments which often involved parents. The programme was also associated with rewards for good behaviour on a group and individual basis. If students felt that they had been unfairly treated there were appeals procedures. There was evidence that this approach was very useful in preventing "exclusions" from school, since it provided a means of dealing with

---

3. In the United Kingdom, pastoral care refers to that aspect of school life concerned with the students' general non-academic well-being.

poor behaviour before it crossed the threshold of unacceptability.

The benefits of a whole-school approach are also evident in decisions about student allocation to groups. For example, in a particularly effective UK school careful attention was given to allocating students to tutor groups so that they would be with other tolerant students and also more accepting teachers. The learning support team in the school also provided a safe haven for students with disabilities, difficulties and disadvantages which was extensively used at recess times. A secondary school in Colorado ran the school within a school called "Choice". This alternative provision, housed in the same school building, gave students more control over their curriculum and teachers reported that it had proved very effective for students, including those with disabilities, who struggled with the structure of the regular school.

4.9 Curriculum development

Curriculum development is another key area in sustaining inclusion and meeting diversity. In Australia for instance, the National Strategy for Equity in Schooling (1994) identified curriculum and assessment as key areas for development for special needs students. In New South Wales, outcomes based education (a structured approach to education stressing the outcomes students should achieve in making progress through the curriculum) has been emphasised and the State's Board of Studies has developed generic life-skills courses to complement the key learning areas of the regular curriculum and to help in the development of individual education programmes. In the United Kingdom and Canadian examples special needs students follow the standard curriculum and teachers make the necessary adjustments for them. In Colorado, a federally funded "systems change project" (Supporting Inclusive Learning Communities) was being used to improve schools through changes in the way they were functioning via action research methods. Progress towards agreed goals is reviewed monthly. In one high school, affective education was part of the curriculum for students with disabilities, difficulties and disadvantages, and covered areas such as socio-emotional development and conflict management. Life-skills and functional independence were also stressed for those with severe learning disabilities.

The use of teachers' time has also been subject to change where inclusive schooling has been effectively implemented. In Italy, for example, primary teachers work on modules comprising two teachers per three classes or three teachers per four classes, with each teacher taking responsibility for a cluster of subjects for two or three years. This approach offers the possibility of providing coherence in curriculum planning for diversity, and enables the teachers to follow students' progress over an extended period.

A key feature of curriculum planning is the provision of teaching materials. In no country was this carried out comprehensively through central services or via private sector publishers, and teachers were left to develop their own supplementary materials. In the United Kingdom, for example, teachers supplemented the regular curriculum with additional resource material especially prepared for each curriculum subject, which allowed for classroom based differentiated teaching. These materials were made accessible to all teachers in the school.

4.10 Classroom organisation

In delivering inclusive education classroom teachers usually had the assistance of at least one other adult who might be assigned for students with moderate or severe disabilities, but who would also work in the classrooms more generally. Often these posts were part-time and appealed to certain people, mothers with children of primary school age for example, whose other activities make it difficult for them to take on full-time employment. A common pattern is for the assistant to work in the class with special needs students planning work within the context of the general curriculum. It would be targeted to meet specific needs, with progress being monitored regularly and the plan adjusted in the light of progress made, *i.e.* an application of formative evaluation. Research showing the benefits of small classes for disadvantaged students was noted earlier.

5. CONCLUSIONS

Creating equitable provision for an increasingly diverse student population is a key policy objective for OECD countries. This is an area in which cross-national analysis can be particularly helpful in informing policy development and debate since there are markedly different national approaches to defining and assisting students with disabilities, difficulties and disadvantages. These cross-national differences, which in many respects are greater than the differences that exist within countries, have great potential for improved understanding about what works best for different types of students. These differences, though, make the task of international analysis particularly challenging. The indicators presented in this chapter are the result of extensive international collaboration, but there is on-going work to improve their coverage and comparability. Nevertheless, even with their limitations, the indicators can help raise questions about current policy and practice.

The data presented in this chapter provide some indication of the extent to which countries make additional resources available for students with defined disabilities, difficulties or disadvantages. Countries vary widely in the numbers of such programmes and the proportions of the student population involved. These differences reflect a range of factors, including identification procedures, educational practices, comprehensiveness of provision, and perceived policy priority.

Countries also vary substantially in the extent to which they include students with disabilities in regular schools or in special schools, and whether they mainly use special classes within regular schools or students are integrated into regular classes. This is a difficult area in which values as well as empirical evidence are strongly contested. Section 2 argued that equity considerations lead to the position that, wherever possible, students with disabilities be educated in regular, mainstream schools rather than in separate institutions. The data presented in Section 3 indicate that the same type of child could be in a special school in country X and fully included in a regular school in country Y. It is inevitable that the educational and social experiences of special schools and regular schools will be different, and this could well be inequitable in terms of students' access to post-compulsory education, the labour market and the wider society. Countries which make extensive use of special schooling need to continually monitor how children come to be referred to them, and at the nature and consequences of the provision in such schools. As well, countries that place a strong emphasis on inclusive education in regular schools need an on-going evaluation process to ensure that its objectives are being achieved.

The qualitative data based on school case studies in eight OECD countries identified a number of dimensions that appear to be important in making inclusive education work (OECD, 1999). In broad terms these ingredients are all found to be important for allowing schools to become learning organisations in the sense that they could adapt themselves more easily and quickly to a wide diversity of student needs, including those with severe disabilities. The resultant flexible provision can provide additional support to all students in the school, and Manset and Semmel (1997) have shown how non-disabled students also benefit from this extra support.

Countries provide considerable additional resources for special education needs and this may be seen as positive discrimination aiding the goal of greater equity. For many students these additional resources can be quite substantial. Using student-teacher ratios as a proxy of costs indicates that students with disabilities in special schools are provided with at least twice the resources of their non-disabled peers in regular schools. Effective inclusive provision requires that these resources are maintained in regular schools which enrol students with disabilities. One thing is clear. If extensive and expensive provision is made in special schools, the skills of the staff concerned cannot at the same time be used in regular education. For instance, in Italy where there are very few special schools, the use of team-teaching in regular schools with disabled students has improved the resources available to all students. Introducing such reforms is of course not straightforward, but the steady accumulation of experience from OECD countries is showing how it can be done.

Despite these encouraging results, there is still a great deal more work ahead. National databases are often inadequate for more sophisticated analyses, especially in regard to linking types and costs of provision to outcomes measures for students with disabilities, difficulties and disadvantages. The OECD is working with member countries to help strengthen the information and research base in this vital policy area.

References

BRESSOUX, P. (1993), "Les performances des écoles et des classes. Le cas des acquisitions en lecture", *Éducation et Formations*, p. 30.

BRIGHOUSE, M. (2000), *School Choice and Social Justice*, Oxford University Press, Oxford.

CRAHAY, M. (2000), *L'École peut-elle être juste et efficace?*, De Boeck, Bruxelles.

DEMEUSE, M., CRAHAY, M. and **MONSEUR, C.** (2001), "Efficiency and equity", in W. Hutmacher, D. Cochrane and N. Bottani (eds.), *In Pursuit of Equity in Education – Using International Indicators to Compare Equity Policies*, Kluwer, Dordrecht.

EVANS, P., BRONHEIM, S., BYNNER, J., KLASEN, S., MAGRAB, P. and **RANSON, S.** (2002), "Social exclusion and students with special educational needs", in A. Kahn and S. Kamerman (eds.), *Beyond Child Poverty: The Social Exclusion of Children*, The Institute for Child and Family Policy at Columbia University, New York.

HUTMACHER, W., COCHRANE, D. and **BOTTANI, N.** (eds.) (2001), *In Pursuit of Equity in Education – Using International Indicators to Compare Equity Policies*, Kluwer, Dordrecht.

LEMONS, J.A. *et al.* (2001), "Very low birth weight outcomes of the National Institute of Child Health and Human Development neonatal research network, January 1995 through December 1996", *Pediatrics*, Vol. 107, No. 1.

MAGRAB, P. (1999), "Training professionals to work in inclusive settings", in OECD, *Inclusive Education at Work: Including Students with Disabilities in Mainstream Schools*, Paris.

MANSET, G. and **SEMMEL, M.** (1997), "Are inclusive programmes for students with mild disabilities effective? A comparative review of model programmes", *Journal of Special Education*, Vol. 31, No. 2, pp.155-180.

MARCHESI, A. (1997), "Quality for all: some comments about inclusive schools from Spanish educational reform", in OECD, *Implementing Inclusive Education*, Paris.

MITTLER, P. (1993), "Childhood disability: a global challenge", in P. Mittler, R. Brouillette and D. Harris (eds.), *World Yearbook of Education 1993: Special Educational Needs*, Kogan Page, London.

NYE, B. (2001), "The long term effects of small classes in the early grades: lasting benefits in mathematics achievement at grade 9", *Journal of Experimental Education*, Vol. 69, pp. 245-258.

OECD (1993), "Access, participation and equity", Document, Paris.

OECD (1999), *Inclusive Education at Work: Including Students with Disabilities in Mainstream Schools*, Paris.

OECD (2000), *Special Needs Education – Statistics and Indicators*, Paris.

OECD (2001a), *Investing in Competencies for All*, Communiqué of the Education Committee at Ministerial Level, 3-4 April, Paris.

OECD (2001b), *Education at a Glance: OECD Indicators* 2001, Paris.

OECD (2003, forthcoming), *Students with Disabilities, Difficulties and Disadvantages, Statistics and Indicators for Curriculum Access and Equity*, Paris.

RAWLS, J. (1971), *A Theory of Justice*, Harvard University Press, Cambridge, Mass.

SEN, A. (1992), *Poverty Re-examined*, Harvard University Press, Cambridge, Mass.

THURLOW, M. (1997), "Standards and assessment in the United States: including students with disabilities in public accountability systems", in OECD, *Implementing Inclusive Education*, Paris.

CHAPTER 1

DIVERSITY, INCLUSION AND EQUITY:
INSIGHTS FROM SPECIAL NEEDS PROVISION

APPENDIX: Allocations of categories of students with disabilities, difficulties and disadvantages included in country resource definitions, 1999

Country categories of students to whom additional resources are allocated:

	Disabilities (cross-national category A)[1]	Difficulties (cross-national category B)[2]	Disadvantages (cross-national category C)[3]
Belgium (Flemish Community)	– Minor mental handicap – Moderate or serious mental handicap – Physical handicap – Protracted illness – Visual handicap – Auditory handicap – Support at home for temporarily ill children	– Serious emotional and/or behavioural problems – Serious learning disabilities – Extending care – Remedial teaching	– Educational priority policy – Reception classes for non-Dutch speakers – Travelling children – Children placed in a sheltered home by juvenile court – More favourable teacher/pupil ratios in the Brussels region – Additional resources for schools in some municipalities around Brussels and at the linguistic border between the Flemish and Walloon regions
Canada (Alberta)	– Severe mental disability – Severe multiple disability – Severe physical/medical disability – Deafness – Blindness – Severe communications disorder – Mild mental disability – Moderate mental disability – Mild/moderate hearing disability – Mild/moderate visual disability – Mild/moderate communication disability – Mild/moderate physical/medical disability – Mild/moderate multiple disability	– Severe emotional/behavioural disability – Mild/moderate emotional/behavioural disability – Learning disability – Gifted and talented	
Canada (New Brunswick)	– Communicational – Intellectual – Physical – Perceptual – Multiple	– Behavioural exceptionalities	– Immigrant
Canada (Saskatchewan)	– Intellectual disabilities – Visual impairments – Orthopaedic impairments – Chronically ill – Multiple disabilities – Deaf or hard of hearing – Autism – Traumatic brain injury	– Social, emotional or behavioural disorder – Learning disabilities	
Czech Republic	– Mentally retarded – Hearing handicaps – Sight handicaps – Speech handicaps – Physical handicaps – Multiple handicaps – Other handicaps – Weakened health (kindergarten only)	– Students in hospitals – Development, behaviour and learning problems	– Socially disadvantaged children, preparatory classes in regular schools

....

CHAPTER 1

DIVERSITY, INCLUSION AND EQUITY:
INSIGHTS FROM SPECIAL NEEDS PROVISION

	Country categories of students to whom additional resources are allocated:		
	Disabilities (cross-national category A)[1]	Difficulties (cross-national category B)[2]	Disadvantages (cross-national category C)[3]
Finland	– Moderate mental impairment – Severe mental impairment – Hearing impairment – Visual impairment – Physical and other impairment – Other impairments	– Mild mental impairment – Emotional and social impairment – Speech difficulties – Reading/writing difficulties – Speech, reading and writing difficulties – Learning difficulties in mathematics – Learning difficulties in foreign languages – General learning difficulties – Emotional/social difficulties – Other special difficulties – Remedial teaching	– Remedial teaching for immigrants
France	– Severe mental handicap – Moderate mental handicap – Mild mental handicap – Physical handicap – Metabolic disorders – Deaf – Partially hearing – Blind – Partially sighted – Other neuropsychological disorders – Speech/language disorders – Other deficiencies – Multiply handicapped	– Learning difficulties	– Non-Francophone students – Disadvantaged children (ZEP priority zones)
Germany	– Partially sighted or blind – Partially hearing or deaf – Speech impairment – Physically handicapped – Mentally handicapped – Sickness – Multiple handicaps – Autism*	– Learning disability – Behavioural disorders – Remedial instruction*	– Travelling families* – German for speakers of other languages*
	* No statistical data are available, but programmes are provided		
Hungary	– Moderate mental retardation – Visual – Hearing – Motor – Speech – Other disabilities	– Mild degree mental retardation	– Children of minorities – Disadvantaged pupils/ Pupils at risk
Ireland	– Visually impaired – Hearing impaired – Mild mental handicap – Moderate mental handicap – Physically handicapped – Specific speech and language disorders – Specific learning disability – Severely and profoundly mentally handicapped – Multiply handicapped	– Emotionally disturbed – Severely emotionally disturbed – Pupils in need of remedial teaching	– Children of travelling families – Young offenders – Children in schools serving disadvantaged areas – Children of refugees
Italy	– Visual impairment – Hearing impairment – Moderate mental handicap – Severe mental handicap – Mild physical handicap – Severe physical handicap – Multiple handicap		– Students with foreign citizenship (no statistical data available)

CHAPTER 1

DIVERSITY, INCLUSION AND EQUITY:
INSIGHTS FROM SPECIAL NEEDS PROVISION

Country categories of students to whom additional resources are allocated:

	Disabilities (cross-national category A)[1]	Difficulties (cross-national category B)[2]	Disadvantages (cross-national category C)[3]
Japan	– Blind and partially sighted – Deaf and hard of hearing – Intellectual disabilities – Physically disabled – Health impaired – Speech impaired – Emotionally disturbed		– Students who require Japanese instruction
Luxembourg	– Mental characteristic – Emotionally disturbed – Sensory characteristic – Motor characteristic	– Learning difficulties	– Social impairment
Mexico	– Blindness – Partial visual disability – Intellectual disability – Auditory or hearing disability – Deafness or severe auditory disability – Motor disability – Multiple disability	– Learning difficulties – Outstanding capabilities and skills	– Compensatory educational needs – Community educational needs – Indigenous community educational needs – Migrant educational needs
Netherlands	– Deaf children – Hard of hearing – Language and communication disabilities – Visual handicap – Physically handicapped/ motor impairment – Other health impairments (no long hospitalisation) – Profound mental handicap/ severe learning disabilities – Deviant behaviour – Chronic conditions requiring pedagogical institutes – Multiply handicapped	– Learning and behaviour disabilities – Children in vocational training with learning difficulties	– Children from disadvantaged backgrounds
Poland	– Light mental handicap – Multiple and severe mental handicap – Profound mental handicap – Blind – Partially sighted – Deaf – Partially hearing – Chronically sick – Motion handicapped – Autistic		– Social disadvantages, behaviour difficulties
Spain	– Hearing impaired – Motor impaired – Visual impaired – Mental handicap – Emotional/behavioural problems – Multiple impairment	– Highly gifted – Students in hospitals or with health problems – Learning difficulties	– Students with compensatory educational needs – Itinerant students
Sweden	– Impaired hearing, vision and physical disabilities – Mental retardation – Impaired hearing and physical disabilities		– Students receiving tuition in mother tongue (other than Swedish) and/or Swedish as a second language – Students in need of special support (not included in other categories) ……….

Education Policy Analysis © OECD 2003

	Country categories of students to whom additional resources are allocated:		
	Disabilities (cross-national category A)[1]	Difficulties (cross-national category B)[2]	Disadvantages (cross-national category C)[3]
Switzerland	– Educable mental handicap: Special schools – Trainable mental handicap: Special schools – Multiply handicapped: Special schools – Physical disabilities: Special schools – Behaviour disorders: Special schools – Deaf or hard of hearing: Special schools – Language disability: Special schools – Visual handicap: Special schools – Chronic conditions/prolonged hospitalisation: Special schools – Multiple disabilities: Special schools	– Learning disabilities/introductory classes: Special classes – Learning disabilities: Special classes – Learning disabilities/vocationally oriented classes: Special classes – Behavioural difficulties: Special classes – Physical disabilities: Special classes – Sensory and language impairments: Special classes – Students who are ill/hospital classes: Special classes – Others of the group "special curriculum": Special classes	– Foreign first language
Turkey	– Visually impaired – Hearing impaired – Orthopaedically handicapped – Educable mentally handicapped – Trainable mentally handicapped – Speech impairment – Chronically ill	– Gifted and talented	
United Kingdom	– Children with statements (records) of special educational needs	– Children with special educational needs without statements (records)	
United States	– Mental retardation – Speech or language impairment – Visual impairments – Orthopaedic impairments – Other health impairments – Deaf/blindness – Multiple disabilities – Hearing impairments – Autism – Traumatic brain injury – Developmental delay	– Emotional disturbance – Specific learning disability	– Title I – Disadvantaged students

1. Definition of CATEGORY A: Refers to educational needs of students where there is substantial normative agreement – such as blind and partially sighted, deaf and partially hearing, severe and profound mental handicap, multiple handicaps. Typically, adequate measuring instruments and agreed criteria are available. Typically considered in medical terms to be organic disorders attributable to organic pathologies (*e.g.* in relation to sensory, motor or neurological defects).

2. Definition of CATEGORY B: Refers to educational needs of students who have difficulties in learning which do not appear to be directly or primarily attributable to factors which would lead to classification as A or C.

3. Definition of CATEGORY C: Refers to educational needs of students which are considered to arise primarily from socio-economic, cultural and/or linguistic factors. There is some form of disadvantaged or atypical background for which education seeks to compensate.

New definitions and changes in national categories, and updates in data, will be reflected in future OECD publications.

Source: Responses by national authorities to questionnaire administered by OECD; see OECD (2003).

Data for the Figures
CHAPTER 1

Data for Figures 1.1, 1.3 and 1.5 are shown on the Figures.

Data for Figure 1.2

Percentages of students in compulsory education receiving additional resources for defined disabilities, by location, 1999

	Special schools	Special classes in regular schools	Regular classes
Belgium (Fl.)	96.8	0.0	3.2
Canada (NB)	0.0	0.0	100.0
Czech Republic	89.1	2.6	8.3
Finland	57.5	34.9	7.5
France	70.3	17.2	12.5
Germany[1]	83.6	0.0	16.4
Italy	1.7	0.2	98.1
Japan	23.2	56.0	20.8
Luxembourg	58.7	1.3	40.1
Mexico	32.2	11.8	56.1
Netherlands	82.4	0.0	17.7
Spain[1]	16.5	0.0	83.5
Sweden	57.7	0.0	42.4
United Kingdom[2]	35.1	0.0	64.9
United States	4.3	22.3	73.4

1. Students in special classes are included in special schools.
2. Students in special classes are included in regular classes.
Source: Based on the classifications (category A) in the Appendix. For further details see OECD (2003).

Data for Figure 1.4

Percentages of students in compulsory education receiving additional resources for defined difficulties, by location, 1999

	Special schools	Special classes in regular schools	Regular classes
Belgium (Fl.)	12.7	0.0	87.4
Canada (NB)	0.0	0.0	100.0
Czech Republic	12.6	14.8	72.6
Finland	5.9	4.2	89.9
France	0.0	100.0	0.0
Germany[1]	88.1	0.0	11.9
Luxembourg	9.7	22.1	68.2
Mexico	1.9	10.3	87.8
Netherlands	52.7	44.8	2.5
Spain[1]	0.0	0.0	100.0
United Kingdom[2]	0.6	0.0	99.4
United States	3.2	18.4	78.4

1. Students in special classes are included in special schools.
2. Students in special classes are included in regular classes.
Source: Based on the classifications (category B) in the Appendix. For further details see OECD (2003).

Data for Figure 1.6

Percentages of students in compulsory education receiving additional resources for defined disadvantages, by location, 1999

	Special schools	Special classes in regular schools	Regular classes
Belgium (Fl.)	0	2.7	97.3
Canada (NB)	0	0	100
Czech Republic	100	0	0
Finland	0	0	100
France	0	0.5	99.5
Germany	0	0	100
Netherlands	0	0	100
Spain	0	0	100

Source: Based on the classifications (category C) in the Appendix. For further details see OECD (2003).

Education Policy Analysis © OECD 2003

CHAPTER 1

DIVERSITY, INCLUSION AND EQUITY:
INSIGHTS FROM SPECIAL NEEDS PROVISION

Data for Figure 1.7
Number of students receiving additional resources in special schools as a proportion of all students by age, 1999 (%)

Age	5	6	7	8	9	10	11	12	13	14	15	16	17	18	19
Belgium (Fl.)															
Males	1.1	3.9	4.6	6.0	6.8	7.8	7.7	7.6	5.2	5.0	4.5	4.5	4.1	2.8	2.3
Females	0.5	2.0	2.6	3.5	4.3	5.0	5.2	4.7	3.1	3.1	2.8	2.7	2.4	2.0	1.5
Overall	0.8	2.9	3.6	4.8	5.6	6.4	6.5	6.2	4.2	4.1	3.7	3.6	3.3	2.4	1.8
Czech Republic															
Males						4.6	5.3	5.7	6.2	6.5	6.8	5.5	4.3	1.5	
Females						3.5	3.7	3.9	4.1	4.3	4.7	4.5	2.8	1.2	
Overall		2.2	2.6	2.9	3.3	3.6	4.0	4.5	4.8	5.2	5.4	5.8	5.1	3.5	1.3	0.7
Finland															
Males		2.1	2.0	2.2	2.2	2.2	2.4	2.5	2.7	2.8	2.9	0.7	0.4	0.6	1.0
Females		1.1	1.0	1.0	1.2	1.1	1.5	1.3	1.5	1.6	1.7	0.4	0.2	0.2	0.3
Overall		1.6	1.5	1.6	1.7	1.7	2.0	1.9	2.1	2.2	2.3	0.6	0.3	0.4	0.6
France															
Males								3.5	4.3	4.5	4.2	1.5	0.7	0.2	0.1
Females								2.2	2.7	2.9	2.7	1.1	0.5	0.2	0.1
Overall								2.9	3.5	3.7	3.5	1.3	0.6	0.2	0.1
Germany															
Males		1.0	3.0	3.8	4.7	5.2	5.7	6.3	6.6	6.8	6.2	3.7	1.7	1.1	0.5
Females		0.6	1.6	2.1	2.7	3.1	3.6	3.8	4.0	4.0	3.6	2.4	1.2	0.8	0.4
Overall		0.8	2.4	3.0	3.7	4.2	4.7	5.1	5.3	5.4	5.0	3.0	1.4	0.9	0.4
Hungary															
Males	0.7	1.5	2.1	2.3	2.6	2.7	2.8	2.7	2.9	2.8	2.4	1.6	0.9	0.7	0.9
Females	0.4	1.0	1.3	1.5	1.9	1.9	1.9	2.0	2.0	1.8	1.6	1.2	0.7	0.6	0.6
Overall	0.6	1.2	1.8	1.9	2.3	2.3	2.4	2.4	2.4	2.3	2.0	1.4	0.8	0.6	0.7
Ireland															
Males	0.4	0.6	0.7	0.9	1.1	1.2	1.3	1.5	1.4	1.6	1.4	1.1	1.3	0.6	0.1
Females	0.3	0.4	0.5	0.5	0.6	0.8	0.8	0.7	0.8	0.9	0.8	0.8	0.8	0.4	0.2
Overall	0.4	0.5	0.6	0.7	0.9	1.0	1.0	1.1	1.1	1.3	1.1	0.9	1.0	0.5	0.1
Italy															
Males		0.0				0.1				0.2				0.1	0.1
Females		0.0				0.1				0.1				0.1	0.1
Overall		0.0				0.1				0.1				0.1	0.1
Japan															
Males		0.5	0.5	0.4	0.4	0.5	0.5	0.6	0.6	0.6					
Females		0.3	0.3	0.3	0.3	0.3	0.3	0.4	0.3	0.4					
Overall		0.4	0.4	0.4	0.4	0.4	0.4	0.5	0.5	0.5	0.8	0.9	0.8		
Mexico															
Males	2.4	1.8	1.3	1.3	1.3	1.2	1.1	1.0	0.8	0.6	0.6	0.4	0.4	0.5	1.2
Females	2.4	1.7	1.2	1.2	1.2	1.2	1.0	0.9	0.6	0.5	0.5	0.2	0.2	0.2	0.7
Overall	2.4	1.8	1.3	1.3	1.3	1.2	1.1	0.9	0.7	0.6	0.6	0.3	0.3	0.4	0.9
Netherlands															
Males	2.0	3.5	4.9	6.4	8.0	9.2	9.9	10.3	7.6	6.7	6.0	4.6	3.3	1.8	1.3
Females	0.8	1.5	2.3	3.0	3.9	4.5	5.0	4.9	3.6	3.2	3.1	2.6	2.0	1.2	1.0
Overall	1.4	2.5	3.6	4.8	6.0	6.9	7.6	7.6	5.6	5.0	4.6	3.7	2.6	1.5	1.1

CHAPTER 1
DIVERSITY, INCLUSION AND EQUITY: INSIGHTS FROM SPECIAL NEEDS PROVISION

Data for Figure 1.7 (continued)

Age	5	6	7	8	9	10	11	12	13	14	15	16	17	18	19
Spain															
Males	0.2	0.3	0.3	0.3	0.4	0.4	0.4	0.5	0.5	0.5	0.5	0.8	0.7	0.7	1.0
Females	0.1	0.2	0.3	0.2	0.2	0.3	0.3	0.4	0.3	0.3	0.3	0.5	0.5	0.4	0.6
Overall	0.2	0.3	0.3	0.3	0.3	0.3	0.4	0.4	0.4	0.4	0.5	0.6	0.6	0.6	0.8
Sweden															
Overall			0.9	0.9	0.9	1.0	1.0	1.0	1.1	1.2	1.1	0.7			
Switzerland															
Males	0.7	1.0	1.5	1.6	1.7	1.8	1.9	2.0	1.9	1.8	1.8	1.4	0.8	0.3	0.1
Females	0.3	0.5	0.8	1.0	1.1	1.0	1.0	1.1	1.1	1.0	1.2	0.8	0.7	0.2	0.1
Overall	0.5	0.8	1.2	1.3	1.4	1.4	1.5	1.6	1.5	1.4	1.5	1.1	0.8	0.2	0.1
United Kingdom															
Males	0.8	0.9	1.0	1.2	1.3	1.5	1.9	2.0	2.2	2.3	2.1	0.8	0.7	0.6	0.1
Females	0.4	0.5	0.5	0.6	0.6	0.7	0.9	1.0	1.0	1.1	1.0	0.6	0.5	0.4	0.0
Overall	0.6	0.7	0.8	0.9	1.0	1.1	1.4	1.5	1.6	1.7	1.6	0.7	0.6	0.5	0.0

Source: Data have been supplied by the Ministries of Education.

chapter 2
CAREER GUIDANCE: NEW WAYS FORWARD

Summary 40

1. INTRODUCTION 41

2. CAREER GUIDANCE TODAY 41

3. WHY DOES CAREER GUIDANCE MATTER FOR PUBLIC POLICY? 43
    3.1 It can improve the efficiency of labour markets and education systems 43
    3.2 It supports key policy objectives ranging from lifelong learning to social equity 46
    3.3 It enables people to build human capital and employability throughout their lives 47

**4. FROM DECISION MAKING TO CAREER MANAGEMENT SKILLS:
A POLICY CHALLENGE FOR EDUCATION** 47
    4.1 Career guidance in schools 48
    4.2 Tertiary education 51

5. WIDENING ACCESS FOR ADULTS 51

6. CONCLUSIONS 53

References 54

Appendix: Career education in the school curriculum in OECD countries 56

Data for the Figure 57

CHAPTER 2

CAREER GUIDANCE: NEW WAYS FORWARD

SUMMARY

Career guidance plays a key role in helping labour markets work and education systems meet their goals. It also promotes equity: recent evidence suggests that social mobility relies on wider acquisition not just of knowledge and skills, but of an understanding about how to use them. In this context, the mission of career guidance is widening, to become part of lifelong learning. Already, services are starting to adapt, departing from a traditional model of a psychology-led occupation interviewing students about to leave school.

One key challenge for this changing service is to move from helping students decide on a job or a course, to the broader development of career management skills. For schools, this means building career education into the curriculum and linking it to students' overall development. A number of countries have integrated it into school subjects. However, career education remains concentrated around the end of compulsory schooling. In upper secondary and tertiary education, services focus on immediate choices rather than personal development and wider decision making, although this too is starting to change in some countries.

A second challenge is to make career guidance more widely available throughout adulthood. Such provision is underdeveloped, and used mainly by unemployed people accessing public employment services. Some new services are being linked to adult education institutions, but these are not always capable of offering wide and impartial advice. Efforts to create private markets have enjoyed limited success, yet public provision lacks sufficient funding. Thus creation of career services capable of serving all adults remains a daunting task. Web-based services may help with supply, but these cannot fully substitute for tailored help to individuals.

CHAPTER 2

CAREER GUIDANCE: NEW WAYS FORWARD

1. INTRODUCTION[1]

Two key challenges today face those responsible for career guidance services in OECD countries. In the context of lifelong learning and active labour market policies, they must:

- provide services that develop career management skills, rather than only helping people to make immediate decisions; and
- greatly widen citizens' access to career guidance, extending access throughout the lifespan.

This chapter presents arguments for the importance of career guidance for public policy, and outlines some of the ways that OECD countries are responding to these two challenges. It begins by describing career guidance. The following section sets the scene by summarising what kind of career guidance is being provided today, who is providing it and in what settings. Section 3 explains why career guidance is central to the achievement of some key policy priorities in OECD countries, by helping to improve the functioning of labour markets and education systems, as well as enabling people to build human capital throughout their lives. Sections 4 and 5 then review the ways in which countries are addressing the two above challenges, extending the scope of career guidance services to meet today's wider goals. Section 6 provides a brief conclusion about new ways forward.

2. CAREER GUIDANCE TODAY

Career guidance helps people to reflect on their ambitions, interests, qualifications and abilities. It helps them to understand the labour market and education systems, and to relate this to what they know about themselves. Comprehensive career guidance tries to teach people to plan and make decisions about work and learning. Career guidance makes information about the labour market and about educational opportunities more accessible by organising it, systematising it, and making it available when and where people need it.

In its contemporary forms, career guidance draws upon a number of disciplines: psychology; education; sociology; and labour economics. Historically, psychology is the major discipline that has under-pinned its theories and methodologies. In particular differential psychology and developmental psychology have had an important influence (Super, 1957; Kuder, 1977; Killeen, 1996a; Holland, 1997). One-to-one interviews and psychological testing for many years were seen as its central tools. There are many countries where psychology remains the major entry route into the profession.

However, in most countries today, career guidance is provided by people with a very wide range of training and qualifications. Some are specialists; some are not. Some have had extensive, and expensive, training; others have had very little. Training programmes are still heavily based upon developing skills in providing help in one-to-one interviews. On the other hand, psychological testing now receives a reduced emphasis in many countries as counselling theories have moved from an emphasis upon the practitioner as expert to seeing practitioners as facilitators of individual choice and development.

While personal interviews are the dominant tool, the examples in Boxes 2.1 and 2.2 show that across OECD countries career guidance includes a wide range of other services: group discussions; printed and electronic information; school lessons; structured experience; telephone advice; on-line help. Career guidance is provided to people in a very wide range of settings: schools and tertiary institutions; public employment services; private guidance providers; enterprises; and community settings. It is provided unevenly to different groups both within and between countries. In most countries there are large gaps in services. In particular employed

---

1. This chapter draws upon the national questionnaires and Country Notes produced during an OECD review of national career guidance policies that began in 2001. These, and other documentation from the review, can be found at www.oecd.org/edu/careerguidance. The countries participating in the review have been Australia, Austria, Canada, the Czech Republic, Denmark, Finland, Germany, Ireland, Korea, Luxembourg, the Netherlands, Norway, Spain and the United Kingdom. Using the main OECD questionnaire, parallel reviews have been conducted by the European Commission (through the European Centre for the Development of Vocational Training and the European Training Foundation) involving European Union countries not participating in the OECD study as well as a number of accession countries, and by the World Bank. In total these several reviews have involved 36 countries.

adults, those not in the labour market, and students in tertiary education receive more limited services than, for example, students in upper secondary school and the unemployed. In many settings, career guidance is integrated into something else: teaching; job placement; personal and educational counselling; or providing educational information. Where this is the case, it can have low visibility, be difficult to measure, and clear performance criteria for it can be hard to define.

Box 2.1 **Career guidance: Three long-standing approaches**

Finland's Employment Office employs some 280 specialised vocational guidance psychologists. Each has a Masters degree in psychology, and also completes short in-service training. Many obtain further postgraduate qualifications. Their clients include undecided school leavers, unemployed people, and adults who want to change careers. Clients need to make appointments, and typically have more than one interview. Demand is very high, and it is not unusual for clients to have to wait six weeks for an appointment.

Germany's Federal Employment Office's career counsellors visit schools, run class talks, and provide small-group guidance and short personal interviews in the penultimate year of compulsory schooling. These counsellors have generally undertaken a specialised three-year course of study at the Federal College of Public Administration. School classes are taken to the Office's career information centres (BIZ) where they are familiarised with the centre's facilities; they can subsequently re-visit the centre and book longer career counselling interviews at the local employment office.

Ireland's secondary schools have one guidance counsellor for every 500 students. Each is required to have a post-graduate diploma in guidance in addition to a teaching qualification. Staffing and qualification levels such as this are quite high by OECD levels. Guidance counsellors are teachers, with a reduced teaching load to provide career advice, to help students with learning difficulties, and to help those with personal problems. Career education classes are not compulsory, but are included in some school programmes.

Box 2.2 **Career guidance: Using innovation to widen access**

Australia's national careers web site (*www.myfuture.edu.au/*) contains information about courses of education and training, about labour market supply and demand at the regional level, on the content of occupations, and on sources of funding for study. Users can explore their personal interests and preferences, and relate these to educational and occupational information. In its first seven months the site was accessed 2.5 million times.

In **Austria** three large career fairs are held each year. They cover vocational training, tertiary education and adult education. They are visited by thousands of people, involve hundreds of professional and trade organisations, employers, trade unions and educational institutions, and are strategically marketed to schools and the community.

Canada's public employment services contract many career guidance services to community organisations, which are often seen as more attuned to the needs of particular groups: single parents or Aboriginal people, for example. Some of these organisations focus mainly on career development activities, such as information services, career counselling and job-search workshops. Others have a wider range of education, training and community functions. Some have career guidance professionals on their staff; many do not.

In **England**, the career service at the University of Leicester used to require all students to make an appointment and have a lengthy interview. During the 1990s student numbers grew by 50% but staff numbers in the career service declined. This forced a rethink. Now, a drop-in, self-service system in a careers resource centre is the major initial form of contact. Career development programmes are run in all undergraduate classes with each undergraduate department having a careers tutor to act as a first point of contact. Increased use is also made of ICT-based tools.

In **Spain**, the international company Altadis has a career development programme, built around a database of employees' qualifications and descriptions of existing positions in the firm. Those taking part in the programme are interviewed regularly to assess their competencies and aspirations against future business needs. As part of a planned redundancy programme negotiated with the trade unions, Altadis offers career counselling to employees, and has contracted a specialist outplacement firm to provide this service. The outplacement firm normally employs psychology or economics graduates to deliver it.

In **the United Kingdom** call centre technology is being used to widen adults' access to education. The service, *learndirect*, provides both information and more extensive career advice to callers. The staff of the service have relevant qualifications at one of three levels, depending upon the nature of their work, and can call upon an online database of information on over half a million education and training courses. Over four million people have called the national advice line since it was established in 1998. The help line is open between 8.00 and 22.00, 365 days a year.

3. WHY DOES CAREER GUIDANCE MATTER FOR PUBLIC POLICY?

3.1 It can improve the efficiency of labour markets and education systems

Evaluation studies, referred to in Box 2.3, show that career guidance can increase job exploration and information search activities. For such reasons, labour economists and labour market policy makers have long recognised that it can help improve labour market efficiency (Ginzberg, 1971; Killeen, White and Watts, 1992; Rosen, 1995; Watt, 1996; Autor, 2001; Woods and Frugoli, 2002). This recognition largely rests upon the value of information in improving labour market transparency and flexibility. It also rests upon higher allocative efficiency as the result of a better match between individual talents and qualifications on the one hand and the skills and qualifications demanded by employers on the other. In principle, career guidance can assist in reducing unemployment: for example by helping to reduce the incidence of voluntary employment terminations or by reducing periods of job search (thus reducing frictional unemployment); or by encouraging those made redundant to improve their qualifications or to seek new types of work in different regions (thus addressing structural unemployment).

Box 2.3 **Evaluating career guidance**

Outcomes of career guidance: A recent review of the economic benefits of career guidance (Bysshe, Hughes and Bowes, 2002) has concluded that evidence for its positive impact upon short-term learning, motivational and attitudinal outcomes can be treated with a high degree of confidence, and in the case of its impact upon actual behaviour with moderate confidence. However evidence on its impact upon long-term individual outcomes, and hence upon economic outcomes, is very limited. Other reviews of research, mostly conducted in the United States and the United Kingdom (Killeen, 1996*b*; Killeen, Sammons and Watts, 1999; Watts, 1999; Prideaux *et al.*, 2000), highlight a number of impacts that are likely to contribute to national educational and labour market policy goals. These include: increasing people's interest in education and training; encouraging participation in formal and informal learning; positive effects on learning outcomes, including better decision-making skills and better awareness of learning opportunities; increased job exploration and information search activities; and increased motivation to seek work.

A complex evaluation model: One reason for conclusions from evaluation research being only cautiously positive is that the model for evaluating career guidance properly is a very complex one (Maguire and Killeen, 2003). Types of clients and their needs and problems vary widely. The help that they receive also varies widely, co-exists with other concurrent interventions and influences, and is often quite brief in duration. Outcomes, both intended and unintended, behavioural and attitudinal, short- and long-term can also vary widely. Obtaining clear answers about impacts under these circumstances requires large-scale research with complex experimental designs and statistical controls. Such research is lengthy and expensive. To date no government has provided the funds needed to do it.

Data needs for policy making: Career guidance researchers have often concluded that policy makers need strong evidence of the economic impact of career guidance. However policy makers' needs are often for more basic data on inputs and processes: what types of people use what types of services; what these different types of services cost; and what clients think about them. Some countries have attempted to gather some of this type of data. For example:

In the Czech Republic the National Institute of Vocational Education has surveyed the extent to which students in different types of schools use a range of career guidance services and their reactions to them. In revealing, for example, that students rely more heavily upon out-of-school sources of help (parents, employment office counsellors) than upon impersonal sources of help (the internet, career fairs, handbooks) and than upon sources within the school (teachers, school counsellors, school psychologists), the survey provides valuable pointers for future service improvement.

In Finland career guidance services in all sectors of education and the public employment office have been systematically evaluated over the period 2000-03. This has involved extensive surveys of actual and potential clients, of service providers, and of institutional managers. These evaluations have been translated into policy changes. For example wide variation in the level and quality of services in tertiary education has resulted in new requirements in the annually assessed financial contract between universities and the Ministry of Education for a concrete plan to improve guidance services, and for strategies to promote guidance within new study programmes.

CHAPTER 2

CAREER GUIDANCE: NEW WAYS FORWARD

> *In the United Kingdom* regional information, advice and guidance partnerships have been established as part of the government's strategy to improve access to education by adults who are disadvantaged and have low levels of education. As part of their reporting requirements to the Learning and Skills Council, partnerships are required to provide data on the number of clients who are members of specified priority groups (lone parents, or ex-offenders, for example). In one such partnership (Kent) client data are recorded by postcode, allowing access to services to be assessed against a number of socio-economic indexes derived from census data. Sophisticated database software enables client referrals to further education institutions to be matched against subsequent enrolments. This provides a measure of service impact (The Guidance Council, 2002).

There are parallels between the role that career guidance can play in improving labour market efficiency and the role that information plays in improving the efficiency of other types of market. However recent work for the OECD and the European Commission (Grubb, 2002a; Tricot, 2002) argues that for many people, career information – a combination of information about education and training, the content and nature of jobs, and labour market supply and demand – is not sufficient by itself. Policy makers need to find ways to ensure that career information is understood, that people know how to use it, that it is regarded as trustworthy, that it is appropriate to the person's level of career development and maturity, and that, where appropriate, people are supported in relating it to personal aspirations, talents and achievements, and in acting upon it.

Career guidance assumes an even higher profile as countries adopt more active approaches to unemployment and to welfare reform. These normally require the unemployed or welfare recipients to develop proposals for active job search, or education and training, as a condition of continuing to receive income support. This increases the need for personal advice, and for access to information, if such policy approaches are to succeed. In Spain, for example, where adoption of the European Employment Strategy now requires earlier intervention to assist unemployed people, the National Employment Office (INEM) has introduced a much stronger emphasis upon individual action planning in the job placement process. This has required employment office staff to develop new skills. In Denmark, Norway and Sweden, guidance is a central element in locally-managed early intervention programmes for school drop-outs. These safety net programmes are associated with strong evidence of improved labour market outcomes for youth (OECD, 2000). Recent Australian research has suggested that intensive interviewing of welfare recipients, including counselling and personal action planning, can increase social integration through increased participation in education and training (Breunig *et al.*, 2003).

Evaluation research summarised in Box 2.3 indicates some ways that career guidance can help improve the efficiency of education systems, as well as labour markets. In principle, it can help to increase access to learning, and to improve course completion rates. It can assess learning needs and interests, and put people in contact with learning providers so that they enrol in appropriate programmes. Feedback from career guidance practitioners can encourage learning providers to meet the unmet needs of learners and potential learners: for example, by changing their opening hours, modifying their teaching methods, or developing new types of course.

In such ways, career guidance can help to articulate better the scale and nature of demand for learning, as well as its supply, and help improve the match between the two. It can increase the transparency of learning systems, and their responsiveness to consumer demand. In these ways, it can help not only to increase participation, but also reduce dropout rates. American research suggests that comprehensive guidance services can have a positive impact on the quality of students' educational and occupational decisions, and also on their educational performance and the overall climate of the school (Lapan, Gysbers and Sun, 1997).

Lifelong learning has major implications for career guidance, and vice versa. The European Commission has recognised this, making career guidance one of its six priorities in implementing lifelong learning (Commission of the European Communities, 2001). The importance of information and advice grows as alternatives and choices within education systems increase, and as the educational choices and labour market consequences that people face become more complex. Countries tend to put more emphasis upon career guidance as they make pathways through education more flexible and more individualised. Both trends can be strongly observed, for example, in Denmark and Finland during the 1990s. Consumer-driven learning systems require greater attention to the information and advisory systems needed to support efficient decision making by individuals. This increases the importance of career guidance in helping to manage transitions from one level of education to another, and transitions between education and working life. And countries place increased emphasis upon career guidance for adults as they seek to expand the range and flexibility of adult learning opportunities (OECD, 2003). This can clearly be seen, for example in Austria, Ireland and the United Kingdom.

3.2 It supports key policy objectives ranging from lifelong learning to social equity

Policy makers in many OECD countries recognise the importance of career guidance for the effectiveness of their education systems. Countries were asked to indicate their key goals and objectives for career guidance in the national questionnaires that they completed for the OECD review of career guidance policies. They were also asked to indicate the major educational, labour market and social influences that are currently shaping their career guidance policies. Austria saw career guidance as a way to improve the permeability and effectiveness of educational pathways. Finland, the Netherlands and Norway saw its importance rising with growing individualisation and diversification of school programmes. The Netherlands argued that career guidance is needed to support the more active approaches to learning that are important in developing lifelong learners. The United Kingdom saw career guidance as an important tool in its efforts to improve basic skills, which in turn are an important part of its lifelong learning strategies. Denmark, Finland, Germany and the Netherlands argued that it can support the attainment of high rates of educational qualification by youth and adults. Austria, Denmark, Finland, Ireland, the Netherlands, Norway and Spain argued that it can help to reduce dropout rates and improve graduation rates.

Other public policy goals have been identified for career guidance. Policy makers in some OECD countries recognise that career guidance has a role to play in promoting equity and social inclusion. In their responses to the national questionnaire for the OECD career guidance policy review, Denmark and Spain argued that it can address the needs of marginalised groups and of the disadvantaged. Finland, Germany and Norway believed that career guidance is important in supporting the social integration of migrants and ethnic minorities. Germany and Ireland argued that career guidance can support the integration of the disadvantaged and the poorly qualified in education, and, together with Spain, in employment. Canada argued that it can address growing polarisation in the labour market. The Netherlands and Spain believed that career guidance can support rising female labour force participation. Austria, Germany and Norway argued that it can help to address gender segmentation in the labour market.

Educational qualifications and employment are important determinants of social mobility: access to them is a key indicator of social equity. Career guidance attempts to maximise the use that people make of their talents, regardless of their gender, social background or ethnic origin. Disadvantaged groups are likely to be less familiar with key educational and labour market information than more advantaged groups. They may be less confident in, skilled in, or used to negotiating access to, complex learning systems. They may need more assistance in finding opportunities that can maximise their talents, and in overcoming barriers to accessing these opportunities. It is significant that many OECD countries have initiated career guidance programmes targeted at disadvantaged groups, or have required services to meet specific targets for access to career guidance by such groups. This has been a strong motivation for recent guidance initiatives for young people and adults in the United Kingdom, and for the *action locale pour jeunes* programmes established for unemployed youth in Luxembourg. However the extent to which career guidance actually contributes to such equity objectives remains an open question in most countries, given the paucity of data on client access to and outcomes from services.

3.3 It enables people to build human capital and employability throughout their lives

Important additional arguments in support of career guidance are found in recent OECD work on human capital (OECD, 2002). This points out that less than half of earnings variation in OECD countries can be accounted for by educational qualifications and readily measurable skills. It argues that a large part of the remainder may be explained by people's ability to build, manage and deploy their skills. This wider concept of human capital sees the planning skills required to develop and implement long-term career goals as a central component of human capital. It sees a wider concept of career guidance – focusing on the development of career management skills, not just upon immediate decision making – as a key policy tool for developing such skills.

Recent thinking about the concept of employability as a tool of labour market policy leads to similar conclusions. There is increasing interest in OECD countries in the notion of employability as a key tool of labour market management: for example, developing employability is now at the heart of the European Employment Strategy (Gazier, 1999). The concept has several interpretations. One focuses on the importance of replacing passive unemployment benefits with active approaches to assisting unemployed people: intervening early in the cycle of unemployment; and requiring individual action plans to be constructed that involve job search, education and training. Another definition places greater emphasis upon the individual, stressing the ability to find and keep a job, and the personal capacity to adapt to a changing labour market and new job requirements. This approach

to the notion of employability within labour market theory strikes strong chords with the approach to human capital found in recent OECD work. Both cases point to the importance of career guidance services having a much broader focus than upon immediate decision making.

Career guidance must, then, respond to long-standing challenges within both the labour market and education, and at the same time adopt a broader approach in responding to newer challenges that arise from lifelong learning, from active approaches to labour market and welfare policy, and from the central role that career management skills appear to play in the formation and use of human capital and in the development of employability.

In its 2001 response to the European Commission's *Memorandum on Lifelong Learning*, France referred to the need for career guidance services to move away from the logic of education, training and occupational selection-allocation, and to move towards the logic of enabling continuous construction of choices and decisions. CEDEFOP (2002) has described this as the key organising idea for the direction of future changes in career guidance services. OECD countries must grapple with how to translate such an objective into the reality of concrete policies, service delivery, training programmes and funding mechanisms. The remainder of this chapter describes some of the specific challenges that they face, and how they are confronting them.

4. FROM DECISION MAKING TO CAREER MANAGEMENT SKILLS: A POLICY CHALLENGE FOR EDUCATION

Traditionally the focus of career guidance in schools has been to help students with the decisions that they face immediately upon leaving school: finding an apprenticeship; choosing a course of tertiary study; or selecting a job. This has resulted in services concentrating upon providing information and one-to-one interviews just before the point of leaving school. If *all* young people need to develop career management and planning skills, an approach based upon doing this through personal interviews is an expensive one, whatever its value in dealing with the immediate decision-making needs of *some* young people. In practice the traditional approach means that many young people may miss out, or that services may tend to become superficial and standardised.

The traditional approach has also resulted in career guidance having a relatively minor role in many countries' tertiary education systems, where it seems to be assumed that students have made a career choice before they enrol. Where they exist, tertiary education services have tended to concentrate upon job search and placement and personal counselling, rather than developing career management skills.

4.1 Career guidance in schools

If career guidance is both to develop important skills for life and work and to assist with immediate decisions, there are significant implications for schools. First, they must adopt a learning-centred approach, over and above an information and advice approach. This means building career education into the curriculum. The Appendix shows wide variation in the extent to which career education is included in the school curriculum in OECD countries. In some countries – for example, Ireland and Luxembourg – it is neither mandatory nor included in overall curriculum frameworks. In other cases it is included in curriculum frameworks as an optional element. Where it is included in the curriculum, the ways in which it is delivered (as a separate subject or integrated into other subjects), the time devoted to it, and the school grades in which it is delivered can vary widely from school to school within a country, as well as between countries.

Second, schools must take a developmental approach, tailoring the content of career education and guidance to the developmental stages that students find themselves in, and including career education classes and experiences throughout schooling, not just at one point.

Third, schools need to adopt a more student-centred approach through, for example, incorporating learning from and reflecting upon experience, self-directed learning methods, and learning from significant others such as employers, parents, alumni and older students.

Fourth, they must incorporate a universal approach, with career education and guidance forming part of the education of all students, not just those in particular types of school or programme.

The experiences of countries that are trying to move towards the type of model outlined above show that a number of difficult issues arise. These include space in the curriculum and time in the school timetable: other teachers may resist time being taken from their subjects. This has been the case, for example, in Austria. Also parents can be concerned that time for career education takes time away from examination preparation. This is more likely to be an issue in upper secondary than in lower secondary education. However in Ireland, a competitive examination at the end of the first stage of secondary education has been a factor acting against the introduction of career education in the lower secondary school curriculum.

One answer to this has been to integrate career education into other school subjects. This can be done, as for example in the Czech Republic, through a detailed mapping of objectives against existing curriculum content so that in principle both are taught at once. Another option, which is adopted in Austria, is to include career guidance in the class time for another subject, but for time in reality to be taken away from the teaching of that subject. Whichever model is adopted, problems of teacher training and motivation are commonly reported for the integrated delivery model. Often teachers do not receive special training to teach career education, and sometimes they have difficulty in seeing its relevance to their normal subject areas (Whitty, Rowe and Aggleton, 1994). Addressing these issues requires a lot of effort to be put into co-ordination within the school: for example to ensure that all areas of the career education curriculum are taught. As Austrian experience shows, this can take a lot of resources and time to do well.

One way that countries have tried to address the need for wider access to career guidance in schools has been to impose a general requirement for schools to provide career guidance, but not to specify how. In Ireland, the 1998 Education Act requires schools to ensure that "students have access to appropriate guidance to assist them in

CHAPTER 2

CAREER GUIDANCE: NEW WAYS FORWARD

their educational and career choices" but does not specify what "appropriate guidance" might be. Not surprisingly, such an approach can lead to wide variation among schools in what in fact is provided (National Centre for Guidance in Education, 2001). Relevant Spanish legislation (the 1990 General Law of the Spanish Education System) is slightly more directive, in that it specifies that career guidance shall form part of the teaching function, that "suitably qualified" professionals shall co-ordinate services, that school services should be co-ordinated with those provided by local authorities, and that special attention should be paid to social discrimination issues.

A commitment to introducing career education also requires decisions to be made on the grades and programmes in which it should be included. The Appendix suggests that the most common approach is to concentrate career education within lower secondary education. There are exceptions: in the Czech Republic, Finland, Spain and Canada (British Columbia and Ontario) it extends into upper secondary education. In Denmark, the Czech Republic and Canada (British Columbia and Ontario) it begins in primary school. The dominant pattern reflects a common assumption that the key career-related decisions are made at the end of compulsory schooling. Such an assumption might have had some validity when the end of compulsory education represented the main point of transition from school to the labour market, or from school to very specific occupational preparation. However this is less and less the case in nearly all OECD countries.

While OECD countries commonly focus organised classes of career education in the compulsory years of secondary education, other forms of career guidance are provided within upper secondary education. In particular, as Figure 2.1 shows, individual career counselling is very commonly provided at this stage. These data, which are available for 14 of the countries that participated in the OECD International Survey of Upper Secondary Schools, indicate that in most countries very many students receive some individual career counseling. However, in most of

Figure 2.1 Percentage of upper secondary students in academic and vocational programmes who receive individual career counselling, 2002

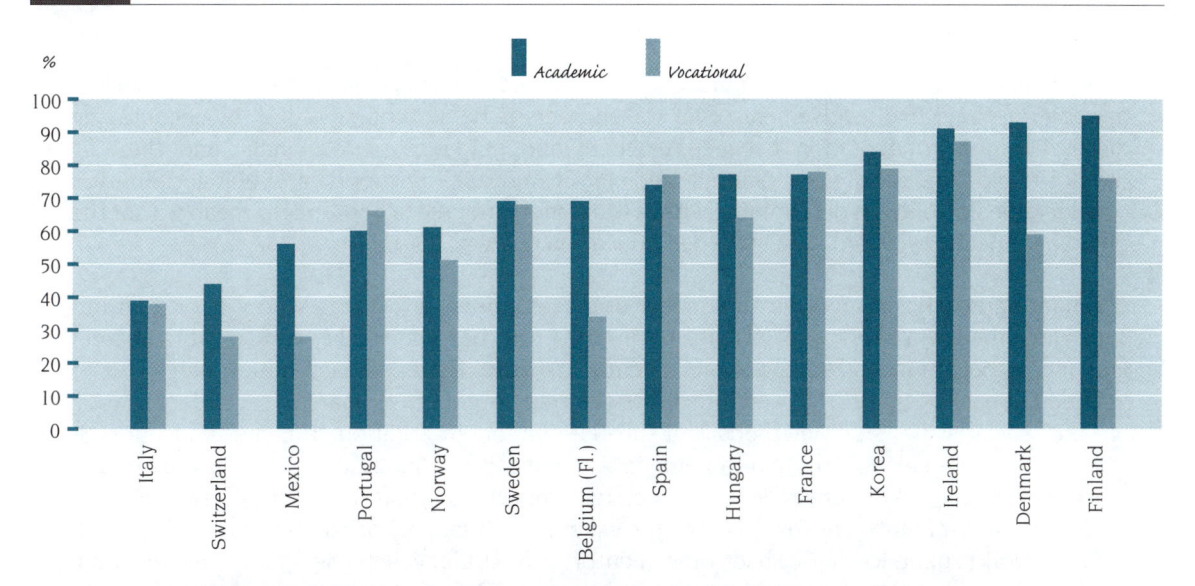

Note: Academic programmes refer to those general education programmes classified as 3-AG in ISCED 97 i.e. those designed to lead to tertiary education. Vocational programmes refer to those classified as 3-BV or 3-CV in ISCED 97 i.e. non-academic (pre-) vocational programmes. However in the case of Italy, Sweden and Finland the reference is to those programmes classified as 3-AV in ISCED 97 i.e. academic (pre-) vocational programmes.
Source: OECD International Survey of Upper Secondary Schools.
Data for Figure 2.1, p. 57.

Education Policy Analysis © OECD 2003

them this seems to be more commonly provided to students in academic programmes than to those in vocational programmes. This appears to assume that young people in upper secondary vocational programmes have made a specific career decision. However like those in academic programmes, these students also face difficult career choices: whether to change track; which specialisation to choose; what type of occupation and enterprise to enter after finishing school; and what long-term career options and further study to contemplate. Such choices become more common as OECD countries increasingly make pathways more flexible through vocational education and beyond (OECD, 2000).

A broad approach to career guidance requires those responsible for school systems, and school managers, to address important organizational issues. These relate to staff training and qualifications; resources; school-community relations; the development of team-based approaches; and the use of a wide range of non-career-specialists (teachers, alumni, parents, employers) in working towards a common goal. As Box 2.4 illustrates, these have implications for the way in which the whole school is organised.

If schools and school systems are to see the development of career decision-making skills, and not just assistance with immediate decisions, as the

---

Box 2.4 "Guidance-oriented" schools

In Canada (Quebec), schools are being encouraged to develop the concept of the "guidance-oriented school" (*l'école orientante*). This is linked to wider competency-oriented school reforms. Personal and career planning is defined as one of five "broad areas of learning" throughout schooling. The aim is to provide support for students' identity development in primary school and guidance in career planning throughout secondary school. This is linked to ensuring that students understand the usefulness of their studies (in languages, mathematics, sciences and so on) and why they are studying them.

To implement this concept, the number of qualified guidance specialists is being increased. In addition, the active involvement of all stakeholders is being promoted, first by encouraging discussion and collaboration between teachers and guidance professionals, and then by developing partnerships with parents and the community. Schools are being permitted considerable flexibility in determining what a "guidance-oriented school" might mean within the broad parameters provided (Ministère de l'Éducation Québec, 2001).

A similar approach, linking a broad concept of career guidance to wider school reform and to wider links between the school and its community, can be seen in the ways in which career guidance is being introduced into some Luxembourg *lycées*. There, the curriculum, which can be included in each of grades 7, 8 and 9 includes the transition from primary to secondary school, life and social skills, study methods and tutorial support in addition to career education. It teaches decision-making skills and career management skills in addition to assisting students to make specific choices. Teachers deliver this curriculum, with support from school psychologists. Employers and parents are involved by, for example, explaining occupations to students. It includes work experience or job shadowing, mentoring by students in higher grades, and personal projects. Luxembourg has commissioned evaluations of these initiatives to assess the impact upon student progression and upon operation of the *lycées*.

goal of career guidance, there are also important implications for the training of career guidance staff. As well as skills in individual interviewing, they will need curriculum skills, community relations skills, skills in managing and co-ordinating teams and, increasingly, ICT skills. Many existing training programmes for career guidance staff have major gaps in these respects (McCarthy, 2001).

4.2 Tertiary education

A wider view of career guidance is also important in tertiary education. Career services are often underdeveloped in this sector, and where they exist, often focus upon job placement or are integrated with personal counselling services (Watts and Van Esbroeck, 1998). The need for career guidance rises as tertiary education in OECD countries operates in a more open and competitive environment, and as the expansion of tertiary participation widens its purposes substantially beyond preparing students for traditional professions. These two trends mean that students have more choices, the link between particular courses of study and specific labour market destinations becomes less direct, and institutions need to become better at monitoring their students' destinations and using their employment outcomes as a key marketing tool to attract new students. All of these imply a shift in tertiary career services towards a greater emphasis upon developing students' employability skills.

Career services in tertiary education have traditionally been much more strongly developed in some OECD countries, notably the United Kingdom and the United States, than in others. However, services are now developing rapidly in a number of countries. In Spain, the Navarra Private University's employment service provides a job placement service for graduates, arranges student learning placements in firms, and organises career fairs that bring employers on campus to provide information. In addition, the university provides a career planning and personal development service for all students on a voluntary basis. Beginning in the second undergraduate year, this involves a web-based self-evaluation tool, personal and employment skills training activities, and meetings between students and tutors. In Ireland, Trinity College Dublin's career service provides assistance through a resource centre, ICT-based tools, and individual interviews. In addition,

it provides a personal and social skills development programme in undergraduate courses. In many cases this is integrated into the normal teaching programmes of academic departments through teaching assistants who have been trained by the career service.

5. WIDENING ACCESS FOR ADULTS

A second key challenge for those responsible for national career guidance policies is to make it widely available throughout the lifespan, and in particular to make it more widely available to adults.

In all countries, career guidance services for adults are far less well developed than are services for youth. Public employment services generally claim that all adults, not only the unemployed, are able to use them to access career guidance. The reality is that very few adults who are not unemployed seem to do so, and that even for the unemployed access to career guidance can be limited and uneven. In all countries, the image of public employment services is that they are services for the jobless. They inevitably concentrate upon short-term employment options, rather than upon longer-term career development and career planning. As a result, in all countries there are gaps in services for employed people who wish to change career direction or to improve their employment prospects, and in services for those who are not in the labour force. Furthermore, given the role that public employment services play in controlling expenditure upon unemployment benefits, it could be argued that a more "arm's length" provision of career guidance to the unemployed is needed.

In some countries – for example in Austria, Ireland and the United Kingdom – there are interesting initiatives to develop new career guidance services for adult education. Many are in their infancy. They have yet to become strongly embedded, and attract far less funding than services for youth and for the unemployed. However they are often more innovative than traditional in character, with strong links to community groups to make them accessible to disadvantaged people. An example of such a service in the United Kingdom is given in Box 2.3. Often, however, these services attract those who have already decided to enrol in adult education courses. Commonly they are linked to particular institutions. As a result they often cannot provide comprehensive advice, and they are often not perceived to act in an independent and impartial way. The latter has become a particular concern in Denmark, where steps are being taken to establish regional services that are not linked to particular adult education institutions. A similar initiative can be found in Austria. The United Kingdom's *learndirect* service is an alternative approach, on a large scale, to the same issue.

As part of their human resource development strategies many large enterprises have internal career development services for their own employees, and purchase outplacement services for those about to be made redundant. Box 2.2 provides a Spanish example of such a firm. However these services are not generally designed to assist those who wish to develop their careers outside their present employer, and tend not to be available for those who are working in smaller and medium sized enterprises. Few examples exist of independent, comprehensive services that are able to meet the needs of all adults, whatever their educational or labour market status.

Providing more comprehensive career guidance services for adults requires governments to address difficult financing problems. In some countries – most notably the Netherlands and the United Kingdom – there have been efforts to create private markets for career guidance. In the United Kingdom, for example, this has been done by limiting public funding to the provision of free "information and advice" and expecting adults to pay for "guidance". So far, these have generally not been a success: in the United Kingdom, for example, the key distinction between "information and advice" on the one hand and "guidance" on the other that underpins funding appears not to be well understood, or adhered to, either by consumers or providers. Markets can be identified for educational guides and other forms of career information, and a limited market exists for outplacement services funded by enterprises. However individuals in almost all countries appear reluctant to pay for career guidance at rates capable of developing and sustaining a market. There are several reasons for career guidance being hard to handle through private markets: both demand and supply are hard to specify and define (even those who provide it are often not able to agree on how to describe the services they provide); it is highly variable in nature; it is often subsumed within other services such as education and job placement; and its benefits are hard to predict or to measure (Grubb, 2002*b*).

The difficulties involved in creating markets for career guidance may mean that the private sector's role is ultimately limited but, whoever supplies the service, the natural fuzziness of supply and demand highlights the need for measures to make things clearer. Thus, governments have a key role to play in making supply and demand more transparent. This is important in helping to ensure that individual choices and preferences can play a significant role in influencing the services offered and how they are provided. It is also important in improving the dialogue between career guidance practitioners and public policy makers. Among other things, this implies the more systematic use of client preference and satisfaction surveys, as well as attempts to increase the diversity of service provision.

In some countries governments have taken the view that free career guidance services should be provided to all adults who demand them, but few countries appear to have been willing to provide sufficient resources to meet the potential demand. This gives rise to difficulties. Bottlenecks and queues can arise, as Box 2.1 illustrated in the case of Finland's public employment service. Some services, for example in parts of Canada, are not widely publicised, partly as a way of limiting demand. This can give the misleading impression that universal access is a reality.

One response to a level of demand that exceeds supply that has been adopted – for example in Finland, Korea, the Netherlands and Norway – has been to look to web-based services. However, these are at best a partial solution. Where, as in Ireland, internet access costs are high, web-based career information and advice is not readily accessible to many adults, and in particular to those with low incomes and low qualifications. And web-based services do not suit the needs of all adults (Watts, 2001), many of whom wish to discuss their problems individually. Nevertheless the popularity of web-based and call centre services (see Box 2.2) indicates that they have an important role. This is likely to increase, even if it is not a complete solution to problems of adult access to career guidance.

In other cases, for example the United Kingdom, governments have attempted to ration services by distinguishing between those that are intensive and those that are less so, and limiting government funding to less intensive services. In practice such distinctions are hard to implement, and appear to be resisted by service providers. Another solution has been to target government-funded services to those considered to be in greatest need (for example: unemployed people; migrants and refugees; those with poor educational qualifications; and low income earners).

All of these approaches raise questions, in a lifelong learning context, of how comprehensive, accessible career guidance services can be made available to *all* adults. Wider debate is required on possible funding models, including mixed models, and a possible future role for individual learning accounts. In addition, debate is required on whether one solution might be for public employment services to adopt a much wider and more integrated role within national lifelong learning and labour force skill development strategies, acting as a key portal to learning and skill development opportunities as well as centres for job placement. This would require extensive changes to marketing and promotion strategies. It would have important implications for public employment services' role in benefit administration, for staff recruitment and training strategies, and for co-ordination between education and labour portfolios.

As is the case with career guidance within education, the approach to career guidance for adults outlined here has important implications for the training and skills of all career guidance staff. Working in community settings, working with groups with special needs, and skills in telephone and ICT-based interventions are among the competencies that need to be more firmly embedded in initial training programmes (McCarthy, 2001).

6. CONCLUSIONS

Education and labour market policy makers in OECD countries certainly behave as if they believe that career guidance can be a tool to help them achieve a number of public policy goals: more efficient labour markets and education systems; more active approaches to labour market policy; lifelong approaches to learning; and a range of equity goals. There are some strong conceptual and theoretical arguments in support of such beliefs. Some of the more interesting of these come from recent thinking on human capital and on employability. The available research evidence offers at least cautious support to such an optimistic view of the importance of career guidance for public policy.

However there is a sizeable gulf between such optimistic aspirations for career guidance and the reality of how it operates and is provided within many OECD countries. Too much of it focuses upon short-term decision making and not enough upon the development of career management skills. And there are large gaps in access to career guidance in most OECD countries: in particular on the part of adults, the employed, and tertiary students. If career guidance is to be a more effective tool of public policy, these will need to be addressed.

Two key challenges have been identified here that need to be addressed if career guidance is to make a more effective contribution to the achievement of lifelong learning and active labour market policy goals. These are: to provide services that develop career management skills, rather than only helping people to make immediate decisions; and to greatly widen citizens' access to career guidance, extending access throughout the lifespan. A number of specific issues that need to be addressed by policy makers, and some of the ways in which OECD countries are trying to address them, have been outlined.

In addition to these specific issues, there are three over-arching questions that need to be addressed in whatever particular approaches are adopted to the challenges that career guidance faces in OECD countries. The first of these is to adopt a more modern approach to the training and qualifications of career guidance practitioners, as gaps can be identified in how well existing training arrangements meet both of the key challenges identified here. An approach to this question, which can be seen in the Canadian Standards and Guidelines for Career Development Practitioners,[2] is to develop

---

2. *www.career-dev-guidelines.org/*

comprehensive competency frameworks as the basis for developing training qualifications, and to ensure that these frameworks can encompass the skills needed by those providing career guidance in all types of settings, in a wide range of ways, and to a wide range of clients.

A second key issue to address is how to improve the ways that services are planned and co-ordinated: between government and non-government services; between education, labour and other portfolios within government; and between the various education sectors. Few countries have adequate mechanisms for doing this. Denmark has recently moved to restructure its guidance co-ordination arrangements within the education portfolio, the United Kingdom has established a national board to co-ordinate the key government career guidance services, Luxembourg has announced steps to improve strategic planning of career guidance services, and Poland has established a non-government national forum for career guidance that involves the key stakeholders. These are positive steps.

A third important step if public policy and career guidance are to be brought more closely together must be for policy makers to improve greatly the information available to them about career guidance. They need to understand better who uses different services for what purposes, how well suppliers are serving demand, the costs and benefits of career guidance services, and what clients think about what is on offer. Improved dialogue between public policy makers and career guidance practitioners can also be a way in which public policy makers can improve the fit between services and policy goals: for example by receiving earlier and improved signals on problems that result from mismatches between student needs and aspirations on the one hand and the nature, size and structure of pathways between education and employment on the other.

References

AUTOR, D.H. (2001), "Wiring the labor market", *Journal of Economic Perspectives*, Vol. 15 (1), pp. 25-40.

BREUNIG, R., COBB-CLARK, D., DUNLOP, Y. and **TERRILL, M.** (2003), "Assisting the long-term unemployed: Results from a randomised trial", *The Economic Record*, Vol. 79, No. 244, pp. 84-102.

BYSSHE, S., HUGHES, D. and **BOWES, L.** (2002), *The Economic Benefits of Career Guidance: A Review of Current Evidence*, Occasional Paper, Centre for Guidance Studies, University of Derby.

CEDEFOP (2002), Consultation process on the European Commission's memorandum on Lifelong Learning, *Panorama*, No. 23, Office for Official Publications of the European Communities, Luxembourg.

COMMISSION OF THE EUROPEAN COMMUNITIES (2001), *Making a European Area of Lifelong Learning a Reality*, Brussels.

GAZIER, B. (1999), *Employability: Concepts and Policies*, Report 1998, Institute for Applied Socio-Economics, Berlin.

GINZBERG, E. (1971), *Career Guidance: Who Needs It, Who Provides It, Who Can Improve It*, McGraw-Hill, New York.

GRUBB, N. (2002a), "Who I am: The inadequacy of career information in the information age", paper prepared for the OECD Career Guidance Policy Review, Paris, *www.oecd.org/edu/careerguidance*.

GRUBB, N. (2002b), "An occupation in harmony: The roles of markets and governments in career information and career guidance", paper prepared for the OECD Career Guidance Policy Review, Paris, www.oecd.org/edu/careerguidance.

HOLLAND, J. (1997), *Making Vocational Choices: A Theory of Vocational Personalities and Work Environments*, 3rd edition, Psychological Assessment Resources, Inc., Odessa, Fla.

KILLEEN, J. (1996a), "Career theory", in A. Watts, B. Law, J. Killeen, J. Kidd and R. Hawthorn (eds.), *Rethinking Careers Education and Guidance: Theory, Policy and Practice*, Routledge, London, pp. 23-45.

KILLEEN, J. (1996b), "The learning and economic outcomes of guidance", in A. Watts, B. Law, J. Killeen, J. Kidd and R. Hawthorn (eds.), *Rethinking Careers Education and Guidance: Theory, Policy and Practice*, Routledge, London, pp. 72-94.

KILLEEN, J., SAMMONS, P. and WATTS, A.G. (1999), *The Effects of Careers Education and Guidance on Attainment and Associated Behaviour*, National Institute for Careers Education and Counselling, Cambridge, UK.

KILLEEN, J., WHITE, M. and WATTS, A.G. (1992), *The Economic Value of Careers Guidance*, Policy Studies Institute, London.

KUDER, F. (1977), *Activity Interests and Occupational Choice*, Science Research Associates, Chicago.

LAPAN, R., GYSBERS, N. and SUN, Y. (1997), "The impact of more fully implemented guidance programs on the school experiences of high school students: A statewide evaluation study", *Journal of Counseling and Development*, Vol. 75, pp. 292-301.

MAGUIRE, M. and KILLEEN, J. (2003), "Outcomes from career information and guidance services", paper prepared for the OECD Career Guidance Policy Review and the European Commission, Paris, www.oecd.org/edu/careerguidance.

McCARTHY, J. (2001), "The skills, training and qualifications of guidance workers", paper prepared for the OECD Career Guidance Policy Review and the European Commission, Paris, www.oecd.org/edu/careerguidance.

MINISTÈRE DE L'ÉDUCATION QUÉBEC (2001), *Prendre le virage du succès. L'école orientante à l'œuvre : Un premier bilan de l'expérience montréalaise*, Direction de la recherche et de l'évaluation.

NATIONAL CENTRE FOR GUIDANCE IN EDUCATION (2001), *Audit of Guidance in Post-Primary Schools 1999-2000*, mimeo, Dublin.

OECD (2000), *From Initial Education to Working Life: Making the Transition Work*, Paris.

OECD (2002), "Rethinking human capital", *Education Policy Analysis 2002*, Paris.

OECD (2003), *Beyond Rhetoric: Adult Learning Policies and Practices*, Paris.

PRIDEAUX, L., CREED, P., MULLER, J. and PATTON, W. (2000), "A review of career interventions from an educational perspective: have investigations shed any light?", *Swiss Journal of Psychology*, No. 59, pp. 227-239.

ROSEN, S. (1995), "Job information and education", in M. Carnoy (ed.), *International Encyclopedia of Economics of Education*, 2nd edition, Elsevier Science, Oxford.

SUPER, D.E. (1957), *The Psychology of Careers*, Harper and Row, New York.

THE GUIDANCE COUNCIL (2002), *Breaking New Ground: Mapping the Territory and Benefits of Career Guidance*, The Guidance Council, Winchester, UK.

TRICOT, A. (2002), "Amélioration de l'information sur les métiers", paper prepared for the OECD Career Guidance Policy Review and the European Commission, Paris, www.oecd.org/edu/careerguidance.

WATT, G. (1996), *The Role of Adult Guidance and Employment Counselling in a Changing Labour Market*, European Foundation for the Improvement of Living and Working Conditions, Dublin.

WATTS, A.G. (1999), "The economic and social benefits of career guidance", *Educational and Vocational Guidance*, No. 63, pp. 12-19.

WATTS, A.G. (2001), "The role of information and communication technologies in an integrated career information and guidance system", paper prepared for the OECD Career Guidance Policy Review and the European Commission, Paris, www.oecd.org/edu/careerguidance.

WATTS, A.G. and VAN ESBROECK, R. (1998), *New Skills for New Futures: Higher Education Guidance and Counselling Services in the European Union*, VUB Press, Brussels.

WHITTY, G., ROWE, G. and AGGLETON, P. (1994), "Subjects and themes in the secondary school curriculum", *Research Papers in Education*, Vol. 9, No. 2, pp. 159-181.

WOODS, J. and FRUGOLI, P. (2002), "Information, tools, technology: Informing labour exchange participants", paper prepared for the conference on Job Training and Labour Exchange in the U.S., jointly organised by the W.E. Upjohn Institute and the U.S. Department of Labor, Augusta, Michigan, September.

APPENDIX: Career education in the school curriculum in OECD countries

Country	Summary
Australia	The location of career education in state curriculum frameworks varies. In some cases it is located within personal development, health and physical education syllabuses; in some within social studies, in some it is integrated into a number of subjects across the curriculum. It is also included in courses in work education and the like which are taken by some students but not others.
Austria	All grade 7 and 8 students must receive 32 hours of career education each year. In most cases it is integrated into other subjects by normal classroom teachers, many of whom have little training for this. In the *Hauptschule* it is provided as a separate subject in around 45% of cases.
Canada	There is very wide variation between and within provinces and territories. For example in British Columbia 60 hours must be devoted to career education and personal planning each year from kindergarten to grade 12 and four credits in this must be obtained for graduation; in Saskatchewan 30 hours of career education are required in grades 6-9; in Ontario a half-credit course in career studies is mandatory in grade 10; in Alberta a grade 11 course in career and life management is compulsory.
Czech Republic	Career education is included in the curriculum for all students from grade 7 through to grade 12. Schools may decide whether to teach it as a separate subject or to integrate it into other subjects. In some 25% of compulsory schools it is taught as a separate subject.
Denmark	Educational, vocational and labour market orientation is a mandatory topic in grades 1-9.
Finland	Career education is compulsory in grades 7-9, and new curriculum guidelines require it to be included in the full basic education. Two hours per week of lessons are provided in grades 7-9, and one hour per week in the optional tenth grade and in upper secondary education. Vocational school students receive 1.5 weeks of career guidance and counselling.
Germany	Schools incorporate *Arbeitslehre* (learning about the world of work) into the curriculum: either in specific subjects such as technology; or more broadly across the curriculum. It is often in the last two years of compulsory school, but may start much earlier. It is less often taught in the Gymnasium than in other types of schools. Classes are supplemented by work visits, and by work-experience placements. It focuses upon learning about the world of work, rather than upon self-awareness and the development of career planning skills.
Ireland	Career education is not mandatory. In upper secondary education two programmes which together account for around 24% of students – the Leaving Certificate (Vocational) and the Leaving Certificate (Applied) – include career education modules.
Korea	Career education is currently being introduced into the school curriculum. "Employment and career" can be included as an elective "extra-curricular" subject for two hours per week for one semester (*i.e.* a total of 68 hours), both in junior and senior high school. Provinces and schools decide whether it is to be mandatory and how to implement it.
Luxembourg	Career education is not mandatory. However some lycées have begun to implement pilot projects, in which career education can be included in grades 7, 8 and 9 for two hours a week.
Netherlands	"Orientation towards learning and working" is included in the upper forms of all general subjects, and "orientation towards the sector" in all vocational subjects, within pre-vocational education. Within general education "orientation on continued education" is an optional component within the so-called "free space" periods.
Norway	Within the curriculum, the goal is that "educational and vocational guidance shall be interdisciplinary topics regarded as the responsibility of the school as a whole". Teaching about working life is in principle included in the subject syllabuses for each grade within the national curriculum for primary and lower secondary schools, but it tends to be phrased in very general terms. In practice, the main focus is from grade 8 and the extent of such delivery varies considerably: it is estimated that on average it amounts to only perhaps 6 hours in grade 8, 8 in grade 9, and 10 in grade 10, largely concentrated in social studies.
Spain	One class hour per week of guidance is included in compulsory secondary education and in the two years of baccalaureate upper secondary education. Upper secondary vocational education students take a "vocational training and guidance" module for 65 class hours per year.
United Kingdom	Since 1997 career education has been a mandatory part of the national curriculum in England for the 14-16 year-old age group, although its extent and content have not been specified and schools have adopted widely differing approaches. Early in 2003 the government announced that career education is to be provided from age 11, and issued guidelines on the learning outcomes to be achieved as part of it.

Source: National questionnaires and Country Notes from the OECD career guidance policy review.

Data for the Figure
CHAPTER 2

Data for Figure 2.1
Percentage of upper secondary students in academic and vocational programmes who receive individual career counselling, 2002

	Academic	Vocational
Belgium (Fl.)	69	34
Denmark	93	59
Finland	95	76
France	77	78
Hungary	77	64
Ireland	91	87
Italy	39	38
Korea	84	79
Mexico	56	28
Norway	61	51
Portugal	60	66
Spain	74	77
Sweden	69	68
Switzerland	44	28

Note: Academic programmes refer to those general education programmes classified as 3-AG in ISCED 97 *i.e.* those designed to lead to tertiary education. Vocational programmes refer to those classified as 3-BV or 3-CV in ISCED 97 *i.e.* non-academic (pre-) vocational programmes. However in the case of Italy, Sweden and Finland the reference is to those programmes classified as 3-AV in ISCED 97 *i.e.* academic (pre-) vocational programmes.

Source: OECD International Survey of Upper Secondary Schools.

chapter 3
CHANGING PATTERNS OF GOVERNANCE IN HIGHER EDUCATION

Summary	60
1. INTRODUCTION	61
2. INSTITUTIONAL AUTONOMY	62
3. FUNDING	65
4. QUALITY ASSESSMENT	69
5. INSTITUTIONAL GOVERNANCE	71
6. INSTITUTIONAL LEADERSHIP	73
7. CONCLUSIONS	75
References	76
Appendix: Country details on aspects of university autonomy	77

CHAPTER 3

CHANGING PATTERNS OF GOVERNANCE IN HIGHER EDUCATION

SUMMARY

Around the world higher education is under pressure to change. It is growing fast and its contribution to economic success is seen as vital. The universities and other institutions are expected to create knowledge; to improve equity; and to respond to student needs – and to do so more efficiently. They are increasingly competing for students, research funds and academic staff – both with the private sector and internationally. In this more complex environment direct management by governments is no longer appropriate. How can the governance of higher education institutions assure their independence and dynamism while promoting key economic and social objectives?

New approaches to governance in OECD countries combine the authority of the State and the power of markets in new ways. Institutions are gaining greater freedom to run their own affairs. Public funds are allocated in "lump-sum" form, and funding from students and business is increasingly encouraged. In exchange for autonomy, governments seek to hold institutions to account, linking funding to performance and publicly assessing quality.

Higher education institutions are having to work hard to meet funding and regulatory criteria and at the same time to strengthen their market position. There is an emphasis on institutional strategy, and a shift in power away from individual departments. External members sit on governing bodies formerly dominated by academic interests. Senior managers are selected for their leadership skills as well as for their academic prowess.

Such changes can create tensions. Higher education institutions need to develop a creative balance between academic mission and executive capacity; and between financial viability and traditional values. Governments have to balance the encouragement of excellence with the promotion of equity. In the knowledge economy the stakes are high.

CHAPTER 3

CHANGING PATTERNS OF GOVERNANCE IN HIGHER EDUCATION

1. INTRODUCTION

Almost without exception, OECD governments have recently been reforming, reviewing or restructuring their higher education systems. Behind such reforms lie profound changes in the objectives of higher education and the challenges that it faces, and with it the character of its institutions and its clientele. It is now well understood that universities and other higher education institutions need to adapt to a more complex environment in which expectations of higher education have changed beyond recognition.[1]

What does this mean for the way in which higher education is run and governed? In the 20th century in most OECD countries, governments exercised considerable control and influence over the sector, to help pursue objectives such as economic growth and social equity. Today, on the one hand, governments have a greater interest than ever in ensuring that educational institutions help meet economic and social needs, given their importance in knowledge-oriented societies. On the other hand, they accept that central planning of knowledge creation, teaching and learning is often inefficient, and that a thriving society and economy require institutions to operate with a degree of independence, while market mechanisms are often more effective than administrators in regulating supply and demand for diverse forms of learning delivered to diverse client groups.

Thus the governance of higher education faces some difficult challenges. If higher education is indeed an important strategic lever for governments in seeking to pursue national objectives, can governments achieve those ends without compromising the independence of universities, or their dynamism in catering for new markets?

This chapter looks at how governments are addressing that question, and at how they are tackling a range of related issues around the governance of higher education institutions. It does so by looking at the degree to which such institutions are able to exercise autonomy and develop their own internal strengths, while still preserving a coherent higher education system overall. Specifically, this involves considering the changing levers of governance in relation to five aspects of the running of higher education:

- first, how much freedom institutions have to run their own affairs;
- second, the extent to which they rely on government funding or can draw on other sources;
- third, the changing ways in which the higher education system itself is subject to quality assurance and control;
- fourth, the strengthening of the governance of the institutions; and
- fifth, new roles for their leaders.

These themes are looked at in turn in Sections 2 to 6 below.

This discussion of "governance" thus encompasses analysis in the broadest terms of how higher education is governed. Governance comprises a complex web including the legislative framework, the characteristics of the institutions and how they relate to the whole system, how money is allocated to institutions and how they are accountable for the way it is spent, as well as less formal structures and relationships which steer and influence behaviour.

Among the many factors that today influence the approaches, old and new, towards higher education governance, a number are particularly important across the five elements discussed in this chapter:

- the debate over whether *markets* are efficient in allocating services such as education, and whether they lead to outcomes that serve the public interest;

---

1. As used in this chapter, "higher education" refers to universities and other tertiary institutions that award degrees and advanced research qualifications. Such programmes normally involve at least three years of full-time study and are designed to provide sufficient qualifications for entry to professions with high skill requirements and to research programmes. In some countries, universities and other higher education institutions also provide programmes that would be classified at a lower level than a degree. Some of the data presented in the chapter relate to tertiary education as a whole in the absence of internationally comparable data relating to higher education. The fact that the concept of higher education is not clear-cut is itself an indication of the complexity of the issues.

- the role of a revised approach to managing public bodies, often called *new public management*, which in other fields is widely credited with the promotion of greater efficiency and responsiveness. In universities, where the idea of "management"-led approaches is sometimes mistrusted, this notion has had difficulty finding widespread acceptance;

- the valuing by many higher education institutions of their *autonomy*. This is not "academic freedom" – although the two concepts are related – but the capability and right of an institution to determine its own course of action without undue interference from the State. Such autonomy is a relative concept, which exists to different degrees in different contexts, and this chapter explores what freedoms higher education institutions do have;

- the important *funding implications* of the huge expansion in enrolments that has turned higher education from an elite sector into one providing for a wide section of the population. Governments that have to fund this expansion and to account to their citizens for the taxes they impose on them are bound to hold institutions accountable for outcomes. Governance of higher education is intimately tied up with funding;

- the growing significance of *market regulation*, through standard-setting and performance monitoring, in higher education systems that are increasingly diverse and risk becoming excessively diffuse. Quality assurance agencies were almost unknown in higher education 20 years ago; now they are widespread; and

- the *international dimension*, which is also growing in importance. Between 1995 and 1999 the number of foreign students in tertiary education in OECD countries grew at almost twice the rate of domestic students (by 9% and 5% respectively – OECD, 2002). The international dimension has also grown through new forms of supply, such as e-learning across national borders and universities opening campuses in other countries. National policy makers now face a much more complex environment in regard to higher education – issues that are already central to national debates now need to be confronted in an international context. These issues have been discussed elsewhere (OECD, 2002) and are not dealt with directly here, but are an important part of the backdrop.

Overall, the higher education reform agenda has involved governments in greater focus on strategy and priority setting and less involvement in the running of the system on a day-to-day basis. In some countries this has included the creation of agencies to monitor the quality of teaching and research, and the emergence of "intermediate" or "buffer" bodies to distribute public resources. Thus, the following analysis is as much about developing new policy approaches, led by concepts such as "strategic management", "deregulation" and "accountability" as it is about influencing the behaviour of higher education institutions directly.

2. INSTITUTIONAL AUTONOMY

In general, universities in OECD countries enjoy considerable freedom to determine their own policies and priorities in a wide range of their activities. Table 3.1 illustrates, across eight areas, the extent of this autonomy in 14 OECD countries. In some aspects, autonomy is particularly widespread – for example, in most OECD countries institutions are responsible for setting academic structures and course content (column 4) and the employment of academic staff (column 5). On the other hand, central authorities commonly have control over certain other features of higher education, in particular, borrowing funds (column 2) or setting tuition fees (column 8), or indeed allowing fees in the first place.

Even within each of these categories of autonomy, considerable variation in practice exists. For example, the freedom to control student admissions can be conditional on meeting various criteria, ranging from the fulfilment of institutional tasks laid down in a budget document (*e.g.* in Sweden) to the admission of a contracted number of students across broad subject categories (*e.g.* in the United Kingdom). These nuances in autonomy are described for each country in the Appendix.

Overall, Table 3.1 shows that universities in three English-speaking countries (Australia, Ireland and the United Kingdom) as well as those in Mexico, the Netherlands and Poland have high levels of autonomy over most areas of their operation. In Austria and the Nordic countries, their autonomy tends to be more constrained, especially in regard to borrowing funds and setting tuition fees. Among the countries listed in Table 3.1, the fewest areas of autonomy are reported in Korea and Japan, at least for their national (public) universities, and in Turkey. In these three countries public universities are essentially treated as part of government, and the State owns their assets and employs their staff. The basic structure of the universities' management, including faculties, staff and student numbers, salaries and tuition fees, is determined by government legislative and budgetary instruments. The main exception, in Korea, is the recent devolution to national (public) universities of the power to set student admission quotas and tuition fees.

Table 3.1 provides a snapshot of the extent of university autonomy at the present time. The broad trend, though, has been for a reduction of direct state control of higher education in most OECD countries. If anything, the process has accelerated

Table 3.1 Extent of autonomy experienced by universities[1]

Institutions are free to:

	1. Own their buildings and equipment	2. Borrow funds	3. Spend budgets to achieve their objectives	4. Set academic structure/ course content	5. Employ and dismiss academic staff[2]	6. Set salaries[2]	7. Decide size of student enrolment[3]	8. Decide level of tuition fees
Mexico	●	◗	●	●	●	◗	●	●
Netherlands	●	●	●	◗	●	●	●	◗
Poland	●	●	●	●	●	◗	●	◗
Australia	●	◗	●	●	●	◗	◗	◗
Ireland	●	◗	●	●	●	◗	●	◗
United Kingdom	●	◗	●	●	●	●	◗	◗
Denmark	◗	●	●	◗	●	◗	●	◗
Sweden	◗	◗	●	●	●	●	◗	
Norway	◗		●	●	●	◗	●	
Finland	◗		●	◗	●	●	◗	
Austria	◗		●	●	●	●		
Korea (national – public)			◗	◗		◗	●	
Turkey				◗	◗		◗	
Japan (national – public)				◗	◗			

Legend: Aspects in which institutions:
● have autonomy
◗ have autonomy in some respects (see the Appendix for details).

1. Data in Table 3.1 are based on responses to a 2003 survey of university governance by members of the OECD's Institutional Management in Higher Education (IMHE) programme. Participation in the survey was voluntary, responses were not received from institutions in all OECD countries, and the IMHE members do not necessarily represent the full range of higher education institutions in the countries concerned. Institutional responses were cross-checked for consistency against each other, and published sources and national experts were consulted in preparing the table. However, the table shows a simplified picture, and countries vary in many detailed respects, as described in the Appendix. Countries are ranked in order of the number of areas in which universities reported autonomy, and alphabetically where the number is the same.

2. "Employ and dismiss academic staff" (column 5) and "Set salaries" (column 6) include cases where any legal requirements for minimum qualifications and minimum salaries have to be met.

3. "Decide size of student enrolment" (column 7) includes cases where some departments or study fields have limits on the number of students able to enrol.

in recent years. Thus, Norway has considerably increased institutional freedom to introduce or remove courses and programmes which form the basis for various degrees (Norway, 2003). In Austria, the Universities Act 2002 has also drastically expanded institutional autonomy; universities are now free to decide on employment conditions, academic programmes, and resource allocation without government approval (Sporn, 2002), and from January 2004 to borrow funds. Recent moves towards greater institutional autonomy are seen even in those countries, such as Japan and Korea, where autonomy has hitherto been relatively restricted. The Japanese government has recently changed the legal status of national universities into public corporations (see Box 3.1), in many aspects influenced by the British reform in 1988 that transformed the ownership of polytechnics from local authorities to higher education corporations. In Korea, "the special act on national university management", which aims at substantially increasing the autonomy of national universities, is currently the subject of legislation.

Despite the broad trends in official policy and government legislation to give greater autonomy to higher education institutions, these changes have often been accompanied by new mechanisms for monitoring and controlling performance, quality and funding. Thus it is simplistic to see higher education reform as always leading towards greater institutional autonomy; rather, it has often substituted one form of influence and control by government for another. In particular:

- Governments have sometimes introduced new funding mechanisms based in large part on university performance on pre-determined indicators. Such changes, and their potential consequences, are discussed in Section 3 below.

- Greater operational autonomy has generally been closely connected with strengthened external assessment of the performance of universities. This has particularly been so in European countries like the Netherlands and Denmark, as well as in Japan and Korea, where state control has generally been strongest. Governments have generally required universities to accept some form of external quality assessment as a prior condition to relinquishing direct state control (Brennan and Shah, 2000). These issues are taken up in Section 4.

In these ways, the price for universities of being given freedom to hire their staff, run their administration, structure their programmes and manage their budgets can be a stricter system requiring

---

Box 3.1 National universities incorporation plan in Japan

In 2002, a study team of experts and representatives from national universities set up by the Ministry of Education, Culture, Sports, Science and Technology published a plan to separate the national universities from the government and give them juridical status. Each national university will be transformed into a "National University Corporation" with the authority to own land and buildings and to hire staff. However, it is also proposed that these Corporations remain basically "national" in the sense that the State will remain responsible for their functions, and provide funds to support their administration. Since the proposed reform is intended to enhance autonomy, it also includes changes in internal decision-making authority. It is proposed that the ultimate responsibility will rest with the university president, who will control internal appointments. The Minister will appoint as president the candidate named by a selection committee with both internal and external members. Since the university's employees would no longer be the subject of the National Public Service Law, more flexible forms of employment, salary structure and working hours will be possible. National universities will also be able to set up and abolish departments and other academic units without needing statutory approval. This plan will be implemented from April 2004, following enactment of the National University Corporation Law in July 2003.

them to account for their outputs or outcomes, as well as new controls on inputs through task-oriented contracts or indicator-oriented resource distribution. The justification for some form of continuing government intervention usually involves arguments that: (i) higher education produces wider social and economic benefits than those captured directly by the individuals involved, and that therefore without government subsidy there would be under-investment in higher education; (ii) equity considerations necessitate steps to ensure that low-income students are not disadvantaged; and (iii) students, employers and the wider society need to have confidence in the quality of higher education qualifications (McDaniel, 1997).

These arguments do not mean that governments should decide everything about higher education. In most countries there is a mix of government influence and institutional freedom, with governments generally involved in ensuring various aspects of fiscal accountability, accountability for the quality of teaching and research, institutional responsiveness, and protecting the interests of vulnerable groups. The ongoing challenge is in getting the balance right by ensuring that governments focus on only a limited number of specific policy goals where the public interest considerations in higher education are clear-cut.

3. FUNDING

The way in which university funding is allocated has undergone extensive change in most OECD countries. Most governments now allocate funds to universities on a lump-sum or block grant basis, rather than by detailed itemisation of budgets. There have also been clear moves toward introducing or increasing tuition fees, output-oriented budget allocation, and performance contracting systems. These changes have paralleled the other aspects of more autonomous, but more accountable, university governance described in the previous section.

The funding changes also need to be seen against the rapid expansion of student enrolments. Between 1995 and 2001 tertiary enrolments grew by at least 25% in half of the OECD countries with available data, and by substantially more in five countries: the Czech Republic (54%); Greece (61%); Hungary (94%); Korea (54%) and Poland (134%) (OECD, 2003a). Total funding has risen from both public and private (household) sources to fund the growth in tertiary enrolments.

However, the rates of growth of public and private funding have tended to differ, which has resulted in a shift in the share of total tertiary funding coming from public and private sources. In countries as diverse as Australia, Portugal and Sweden private expenditure grew much more rapidly than public expenditure between 1995 and 2000, which resulted in declines in the share of expenditure on tertiary institutions coming from public sources: from 65% to 51% in Australia; from 97 to 93% in Portugal; and from 94 to 88% in Sweden. On the other hand, public funding grew more rapidly than private expenditure in some countries, which meant that the share of public expenditure on tertiary education institutions actually increased over this period, for example in the Czech Republic (to 86%), and in Ireland (to 79%) (OECD, 2003a).

One factor in the rising share of private expenditure in some countries can be the growing importance of private tertiary institutions that charge fees. Another factor, as discussed below, is increased or newly imposed fees or charges in institutions that previously were largely publicly funded. This is particularly evident in the higher education component of tertiary education. As well, the basis by which public funds are allocated to higher education has changed in many countries. The net result is that higher education institutions now face a more varied and perhaps less predictable funding environment.

The switch from *itemised to lump-sum or block grant budgets* has been commonplace in OECD countries (*e.g.* Austria, the Czech Republic, Ireland, Sweden and Finland). This represents a fundamental change in governance from specification by a ministry about how money is spent to allowing institutions to decide, within the regulations for public sector finance. In such countries, the majority of recurrent spending for teaching activities, support services and administration is now provided in the form of block grants; however, there are generally separate allocations for research, capital expenditure or specific projects and development (Eurydice, 2000). As noted above, Japan and Korea – which still retain the system of itemised funding through negotiation with the appropriate ministry – are currently implementing reforms to introduce block grants.

By contrast, *funding for research* has tended to become more rather than less specified, with governments aiming to increase the proportion of earmarked funds, whether from governments and funding agencies or from other private sources, at the expense of lump-sum research budgets. The trend towards funding for specified research activities is not new in the United States, where earmarked research is well-established, but it is new in much of Europe. Countries such as the Netherlands, the United Kingdom and the Czech Republic have moved particularly strongly towards earmarking of research funding (Braun and Merrien, 1999). The *specification* of a research grant for a particular purpose can be distinguished from another trend, namely towards the *assessment of entitlement* to research funding based on specified performance criteria. For example, the United Kingdom has developed a very detailed and extensive competitive research funding tool (see Box 3.2).

In the case of block grants for recurrent funding, there has also been a trend towards governments using *formula funding* based on services provided and performance levels. Some recent examples of such changes are summarised in Table 3.2. These formulae are often based on student numbers, and hence in some respects on performance in attracting clients. However, there are also efforts towards linking funding to outputs and outcomes. A number of European countries (Finland, the Netherlands, Norway, Sweden, and the United Kingdom) have incorporated outputs in their funding formulae, by taking account not just of enrolments but of student completion rates. For example, the United Kingdom government specifies target student numbers based on previous levels and current government priorities, and penalises institutions that do not meet them. There has also been a move towards linking funding to medium-term objectives negotiated between government and universities. Such "performance contracting", pioneered by France in 1988, followed by Finland and Switzerland in the late 1990s, and Austria in 2002, is illustrated through the Finnish example in Box 3.3.

Box 3.2 Research funding in the United Kingdom

In the United Kingdom there is a dual support system for funding higher education research. The Higher Education Funding Council for England (HEFCE) and the Scottish Higher Education Funding Council in Scotland distribute funds selectively to higher education institutions with reference to the quality of research as assessed in a Research Assessment Exercise (RAE). The RAE is conducted every four or five years; the most recent was in 2001 and informed funding decisions from 2002-2003. Each institution was awarded a rating, on a scale of 1 to 5* (five star), for the quality of its research in each unit of assessment (academic department) in which it was active. Only the highest rated departments attract funding, and a quality rating of 5* attracts almost three times as much funding as a rating of 4 for the same volume of research activity. As a result, funding for research is highly concentrated by institution and department. In 2002-2003, 75% of HEFCE research funds were allocated to 25 institutions out of a total of around 135 higher education institutions in England.

A second stream of government funding allocated by the Research Councils for specific projects covers the direct costs of those projects awarded. The quality-related funding supports the infrastructure and indirect costs and also provides institutions some flexible resources for their own research.

The UK funding councils are currently consulting on a review of research assessment.

Source: HEFCE (2002).

CHAPTER 3

CHANGING PATTERNS OF GOVERNANCE IN HIGHER EDUCATION

Table 3.2 **New methods for allocating recurrent funding to universities: country examples**

Country	When implemented	Main features
Australia	1988 (and progressively modified since)	• Commonwealth (federal) government funding (around 60% of total revenue in 2001) has two main components: (i) a general operating grant largely based on a specified number of student places in the context of an educational profile of the institution concerned; and (ii) funds for research and research training allocated primarily on a competitive basis. • Resources are allocated in the context of a rolling triennium which ensures that institutions have a secure level of funding on which to base their planning for at least three years.
Czech Republic	1992 (and progressively modified since)	• The major part of funding for teaching activities (about 78% in 2002) is based on inputs (the number of students multiplied by the cost of relevant studies). Around 10% is provided on a competitive basis whereby institutions are invited to submit projects in response to state priorities. The government aims to increase the competitive component to 30% over the next few years. • Government funding for research has two main components: around 30% (research directly connected to teaching) is based on a formula taking into account: (i) the funds raised by the institution for research and development; (ii) the ratio of professors and associate professors to the total academic staff; and (iii) the ratio of graduates from doctoral and master's programmes to the total number of students in the institution. • The other 70% of research funding is provided through a competitive bidding process.
Netherlands	2000	• Universities are funded on the "performance funding model". Thus 50% of the total teaching budget in 2000 was based on the number of degrees awarded in 1999; 13% was based on the number of first year enrolments; and the remainder was a fixed allocation per university. Universities receive separate funding for research programmes. • Universities of professional education (HBOs: *Hoger Beroepsonderwijs*) are allocated teaching funds by a formula taking into account programme characteristics and teaching output (enrolment and completion rates). • The government has foreshadowed plans to merge these two systems from 2005.
Norway	2002	Grants to institutions now consist of three main components: • a basic component (on average approximately 60% of the total allocation in 2002) associated with unit cost; • an education component (approximately 25%) based on results: the number of completed student credits, the number of graduates (scheduled to begin in 2005), and the number of international exchange students (incoming and outgoing); and • a research element (approximately 15%) dependent on performance and quality criteria including: (i) ability to attract external funding; (ii) number and qualifications of academic staff; (iii) number of postgraduate students; (iv) regional and professional policy priorities; and (v) total student numbers.
Switzerland	2000	University funding, which was based on teachers' salaries, student enrolments and cantons' financial capacity, now takes account of the services provided by universities: • 70% of basic funding is allocated according to the number of students enrolled for the legal duration of studies, weighted by academic disciplines; and • 30% is distributed as matching funds to the contributions that each university obtains from third parties (*e.g.* the Swiss National Science Foundation and the Commission for Technology and Innovation).

Source: IMHE and HEFCE (forthcoming); OECD (2003b); Norwegian Ministry of Education and Research (2003); Benes and Sebková (2002).

> **Box 3.3 University performance contracting in Finland**
>
> The Finnish government has a three-year contract with each university that covers objectives, programmes and funding. The contract provides for a government grant in the form of a lump sum to implement the contract, including the goals for master's and doctoral degrees. The budgeting system has been developed to support management-by-results so that the university's goals and appropriations are inter-linked:
>
> - the same three-year period is used both for measuring outcomes and allocating resources;
> - negotiations run from February to April preceding the three-year funding period; and
> - each university documents the achievement of goals in the form of an annual report.
>
> *Source*: Holtta and Rekila (2002).

Another conspicuous trend in the funding of institutions has been government encouragement for them to sell teaching and research services: *contract-based funding*. In general, there appear to be two main types of contract undertaken by institutions: contracts with central or regional governments for specific course programmes or research projects; and contracts obtained on the open market with private organisations (Eurydice, 2000). Contract-based funding is common in the United States and Australia. In Europe, the governments of the Netherlands and the United Kingdom have made the strongest demands for universities to seek external funds, including from the European Union. Other countries, for instance, Ireland, Norway, Sweden and Switzerland "have recognized the need for higher education institutions to remain essentially publicly funded while encouraging them to sell their services on an educational market" (Eurydice, 2000, p. 97).

A further funding issue for higher education, and overall the most controversial, is whether and at what level to charge undergraduate students *tuition fees* (see, for example, Biffl and Isaac, 2002). To illustrate the range of contexts, all higher education institutions in the United States charge tuition fees, albeit at a wide range of levels and many students get financial support or scholarships; by contrast, it is constitutionally impossible for higher education institutions to charge tuition fees in Sweden and Finland. The main argument for fees, based on the private financial benefits of higher education, is stronger to the extent that students form a minority of the age-group and are drawn disproportionately from already-favoured social groups. Yet the practical impetus for introducing fees has been (i) the need to finance the dramatic expansion of student numbers; and (ii) "the political will to encourage self-reliance and consumer choice" (Eurydice, 2000, p. 98). For example, Australia introduced tuition fees in 1989 to both finance expansion of higher education and also ensure that those who benefited from higher education paid a greater share of the costs. A distinctive feature is that payment of the fees is contingent on how much students earn after leaving higher education: students can choose to defer their payment and begin repaying the debt through the income tax system when their income reaches a minimum threshold. By 2001 Australian higher education institutions obtained about 30% of their revenue from student fees.[2] However, only a few countries in Europe (Italy, the Netherlands, Portugal, the United Kingdom and, very recently, Austria) have introduced significant increases in student fees since 1980, while Ireland in 1996 decided that the tuition fees would be paid by the government (Eurydice, 2000; Sporn, 2002).

Fees also relate to other aspects of governance: public higher education institutions in Korea (2002) and to some extent in the Netherlands (1996), have been granted the right to set their own fees in an effort to strengthen their financial autonomy. Both the United Kingdom[3] and the Aus-

---

2. More details on the Higher Education Contribution Scheme in Australia are provided in Chapter 4 (Section 4.2) of this volume.

3. This decision applies to England, Wales and Northern Ireland only. The Scottish Executive has announced that it does not intend to permit variable fees.

tralian governments recently announced proposals to give universities greater financial autonomy by allowing them to vary fees subject to a prescribed maximum.

A further aspect of the growing diversification of higher education funding is direct financing by "third parties", such as industry and private foundations, of research and development in particular.[4] The effects of this phenomenon reinforce those of public funding coming in more of a "contracted" form: in both cases, higher education institutions in effect become more like corporations competing for funding streams rather than being primarily extensions of the ministries that sponsor them. This has some important implications for public policy and institutional governance.

Not being dependent on a single stream of funds increases the autonomy of institutions to plan and shape their own futures. The fact that higher education institutions now are required (or choose to) use a wider range of funding sources (rather than being largely dependent on government) means that they are less vulnerable to sudden shifts (*e.g.* when government priorities change). However, it can also lead to increased uncertainty of resource flows, and in some cases even threaten the very survival of an institution over the long term. In countries such as the United States, where these conditions have long applied, large numbers of higher education institutions have closed over the years due to financial pressures. For other countries, where the growth of non-government funding sources for higher education is much more recent, there are potentially challenging legal and political issues ahead: to what extent, and under what conditions, is the State obliged to continue to financially support higher education institutions that have got into financial difficulties?

An increasing reliance on "third party funding" may shift the balance of higher education resources towards those activities where the commercial possibilities are greatest (De Boer, 2000). Some scholars express concern that lucrative private work pushes away traditional academic activities, and emphasises "applied" compared to "curiosity-driven" or "discipline-based" research. Universities may thus acquire a hybrid of public and private norms and values, which may sit uncomfortably together and at worst tear the institution apart. Such a scenario makes it even more important that those responsible for external quality assurance, and internal management, ensure that higher education institutions continue to serve their wider public responsibilities.

4. QUALITY ASSESSMENT

Almost without exception, increased autonomy over a wide range of institutional operations has been accompanied by the introduction of a more sophisticated quality assurance system based on the establishment of a national quality agency for higher education. This has shifted responsibility for higher education quality from a mainly internal judgement by institutions themselves to an external process of peer review and judgement by others such as quality assessment agencies, and funding bodies. While this is a relatively recent development in most countries, and in many cases still in its formative stages, higher education accreditation bodies have existed in the United States for a century.

The 1990s saw the establishment of a national quality assessment agency in almost all OECD countries; in 1990 they had existed in only a handful of countries. Box 3.4 shows some common and differing features of such bodies in a range of countries.

---

4. It is difficult to obtain systematic international data on private sector funding of research and development, but there are some indicative data. In the United States, industry-sponsored R&D expenditure at 32 public universities that are members of the American Association of Universities doubled between 1990 and 2001 (Vaughn, 2001). In the Netherlands, the proportion of income from contract activities in research-intensive universities rose from 12% to 18% between 1990 and 1999. In Sweden, the share of research grants coming directly from central government declined from around 65% to 45% between the mid-1980s and 2001. In the United Kingdom in 1999-2000 HEFCE grants constituted around 33% of total research funding received by higher education institutions, with other significant sources being research councils (22%), foundations and charities (17%), central government/local authorities and health authorities (11%), industry (8%) and other grants and contracts (10%) (IMHE and HEFCE, forthcoming).

Box 3.4 **National quality assessment agencies: Similarities and differences**

By the end of the 1990s, almost every OECD country had a national agency for the assessment of quality in higher education institutions. They have important characteristics in common. Almost all *operate independently* from government, in principle, rather than being a direct arm of a ministry. Almost all are *funded* by government. Almost all rely on judgements made by *external evaluation teams* mostly comprising academics from other institutions, including in some cases from other countries.

However, countries have also developed some different features in their quality assessment agencies. Many are *set up by governments* (*e.g.* the Danish Evaluation Institute, EVA; the Center of Accreditation and Quality Assurance of the Swiss Universities, OAQ; the Norwegian Agency for Quality Assurance in Education, NOKUT; the Australian Universities Quality Agency, AUQA; the National Institution for Academic Degrees and University Evaluation, NIAD, in Japan; and the Swedish National Agency for Higher Education which has a new mandate to carry out quality assurance); some are *owned collectively* by higher education institutions (*e.g.* the Foundation of Portuguese Universities); others are *independently constituted* (*e.g.* the National Evaluation Committee, CNE, in France; the Quality Assurance Agency, QAA, in the United Kingdom; and the Netherlands Accreditation Organisation, NAO). Yet regardless of how they are constituted, their reliance on the expertise of members of the academic community helps to give them legitimacy.

In some countries there is a *single national quality agency*, in others, *more than one*. An important factor is whether a single national assessment system can be identified: this tends to be the case in countries with relatively homogeneous and smaller systems like the Netherlands and Denmark, but not in Germany, a federal country where there is no single assessment system at the national level, nor in the United States or Mexico, where multiple external assessment systems exist.

In Austria existing quality assurance arrangements applied only to *Fachhochschulen* and to private institutions (which together comprise about 10% of the higher education sector), but they are to be extended to all universities at the end of 2003.

National quality agencies differ considerably in the level and focus of their assessment methods. They may focus on an *institution* (*e.g.* Australia), on a *programme* (*e.g.* the Netherlands), or on a *combination of both* (in most other countries). At each of these levels they may concern themselves with teaching, research or management/administration.

In most cases, reports are made *public*, but not in Italy or Greece, where they are given only to the Ministry, nor in Austria in the case of reports on single institutions, where they go only to the institution assessed.

The assessment is mainly a form of *regulation* and *information* rather than being used for funding decisions. However, in the United Kingdom a specific link is made between evaluation outcomes and *funding* (see Box 3.2 above for the case of research funding). In the countries where funding is based on outputs (see Section 3 above), external quality assessment may be used to verify funding-related information.

Source: Brennan and Shah (2000); INQAAHE (2001); Eurydice (2000).

A key issue is who determines the rules and value systems that underlie the assessment criteria. Potentially, the answer can be "governments", in which case a government that is not directly managing an institution can exert an indirect yet powerful form of control, as the values embedded in quality assurance mechanisms become deeply woven into the procedures and judgements of the institution.

One significant effect of new external quality assurance mechanisms, in combination with increased institutional autonomy, has been to change the distribution of authority within higher education. Academic heads of department who once may have negotiated with ministries for funding find their power squeezed from two directions. First, the chief executive of the institution now often has a more direct influence on external funding sources and internal resource allocation. Second, external review and quality assurance may further reduce the capacity of individual academic departments or staff members to determine their own priorities (Brennan and Shah, 2000). This shift in the internal power structure is explored further in the following section.

5. INSTITUTIONAL GOVERNANCE

The traditional model of governing universities is collegial and consultative in nature, with large and broadly representative bodies and forums open to all academic members of the university. The changes outlined in this chapter have had two main effects on internal governance: a strengthening of the power of executive authorities within the university; and an increase in participation on governing or supervisory bodies by representatives and individuals from outside the university.

In most countries there have been efforts to reinforce the executive authority of institutional leaders (Table 3.3 provides some recent examples). Key common elements have been a transfer of power to the Rector, Vice-Chancellor and other leading administrative figures, and a loss of authority and decision-making power on the part of traditional participatory and collegial bodies. However, the strategies and structures chosen to implement this development have varied widely.

Reinforcing the general loss of faculty power, the increased weighting of "external constituencies" and outside interests has contributed to the strength of executive authorities. The manner in which these are represented varies considerably. For example:

- Recent Dutch legislation, particularly the 1997 University Modernisation Act, split leadership between a Rector with executive responsibility and a President of the Supervisory Board drawn from outside the university. This is comparable to the American model of university President and Chairman of the Board of Trustees (Neave, 2001). Recent Austrian governance reform has similarities to the Dutch reforms.

- In Sweden, the Governing Board has a majority of external representatives from business, industry and regional authorities (usually 8 external out of a total of 15 members). Furthermore, since 1997, the chair of the Governing Board is no longer the Vice-Chancellor but "a well-qualified and experienced external personality" who is not employed at the institution and is appointed by the government.

Part of the aim of bringing external representatives into higher education governance has been to include more people with industrial or commercial experience and thereby hopefully strengthen links to the economy and improve internal efficiency. Other external members have been from local or regional government to reflect greater regional interests in funding, and in the contribution of the higher education institution to local economic and social development (Eurydice, 2000). While such representation tends to reduce the relative power of academic interests, the outside interests do not necessarily predominate. One consequence of this model can be a strengthened chief executive's position by virtue of their greater access to internal information and knowledge.

Pressures to change the traditional models of university governance have become more acute in recent years as public funding has often become more targeted (and in some countries reduced in per student terms), as institutional autonomy has increased and as, in parallel, external performance management and other accountability

Table 3.3 New models of institutional governance: country examples

Country	Year	Main governing body	What changed?
United Kingdom	1988	In the "new" universities (mainly former polytechnics) the main governing body is a *Board of Governors* which generally comprises about 25 members, the majority of whom are external; there is also generally an *Academic Board* which comprises academic staff only.	Established a small Executive Board, half of whom must be from outside the university with experience in industrial, commercial or employment matters. Strengthened the power of the Chief Executive. Subordinated the Academic Board to the Board of Governors in all aspects and to the Chief Executive in some respects.
		In the "old" universities the main governing body is generally a *Council* of 25-60 members, the majority of whom are external, and a Senate comprising academic staff only.	Although the "old" universities were not affected by the 1988 Education Reform Act, the report of the National Committee of Enquiry into Higher Education in 1997 made recommendations about governance which have, in the main, been adopted by them.
Netherlands	1997	*Supervisory Board*, 5 external members appointed by Ministers.	Replaced joint decision-making by Administrative Board and Academic Council.
		Executive Board, 3 internal members including the Rector.	Introduced Supervisory Board, which supervises and appoints members of the Executive Board. The Executive Board is accountable for governance and administration to the Supervisory Board.
		University Council, academic, administrative staff, plus students; mainly advisory function.	University and Faculty Councils became largely advisory bodies for students and employees. Executive strengthened relative to University and Faculty Councils; Dean's power increased within faculty. Abolition of the previously powerful Disciplinary Research Groups.
Austria	2002	*University Council*, 5-9 external members, nominated by the Ministry and the University Senate.	Introduced the University Council which will appoint the Rector, and decide on the organisational plan, budget, and employment structure.
		Rectorate, the Rector and up to 4 Vice-Rectors.	The Rector takes on a senior management function, supported by a team of Vice-Rectors.
		Senate, academic, administrative staff, students; majority of members are professors.	The Senate was retained, but lost much of its power, and is to focus mainly on academic programmes.
Japan	2004	*Administrative Council* with internal and external members.	Administrative Council created to decide on main financial, personnel and organisational issues.
		Academic Council, comprising the university President, heads of faculty, academics, others appointed by the President.	Academic Councils created to decide curriculum, appointment of academic staff. Executive Board created comprising the university President and several Vice-Presidents. Overall the university President gains considerable powers.

Source: IMHE and HEFCE (forthcoming); Austria (2002).

mechanisms have required universities to publicly demonstrate their efficiency and effectiveness. Strengthening executive responsibility can help institutions to sharpen their performance in a competitive environment by clarifying lines of responsibility and developing more of a strategic capacity.

At the same time, such changes can generate tensions within higher education institutions. In the long term, their success will depend on resolving these tensions – since it would be hard for a university to retain a true sense of mission if significant numbers of academics become alienated from the institution. This does not mean removing the competition between the cultures of managerialism and academic values, but rather ensuring that they are complementary rather than counter-productive.

6. INSTITUTIONAL LEADERSHIP

Crucial aspects of the development of more powerful executives in higher education are the processes by which they are appointed and the qualities of the individuals concerned. As pressure mounts to make institutions more accountable, to develop better linkages with the wider society, and to raise external funds, their leaders need to be more than outstanding academics.

In many countries, the tradition has been to elect university leaders to ensure that they represent the constituency – especially the academic one – of the university. As shown in Table 3.4, although election of university leaders still continues in a number of countries, the trend seems to be moving towards appointment, often by a board with a majority of external members. Legislative changes in Austria, Denmark and Norway introducing new appointment systems, represent recent examples of this trend. In Norway, however, appointment remains an exception from normal procedure and has only been used to date in state university colleges and institutes of the arts.

The change towards appointment rather than election is a crucial part of the redefinition of the relationship between the chief executive and others within the institution. An appointed rather than elected chief executive may find it easier to implement major changes that cut across vested interests. Nevertheless the process of appointment is vital to ensure that the institutional leader has credibility within the institution.

Indicators of the changed roles and expectations of institutional leaders are found in the language of recruitment advertisements, for example:

"We are looking for an outstanding individual who combines the ability to inspire and lead with a clear vision of the future direction of higher education, both nationally and internationally. The successful person will have the drive, personality and determination to develop the University to match that vision." (United Kingdom University)

"We need a leader who, together with me [the Chair of Council], the board and a large number of qualified staff members, can lead the activities into a new millennium. You should have good knowledge about industry, business and authorities within the [institution's] sectors of activity and a good anchorage in the science fields covered ... A wide network of contacts and experience from leading large knowledge-producing organisations are also important, as well as the ability to inspire." (Swedish University)

Nevertheless, a strong academic background continues to figure prominently in leadership appointments. A survey in four of the countries that appoint their university leaders (the Netherlands, Sweden, the United Kingdom and the United States) found that:

"Despite extensive changes in university organization, key structural elements, particularly those which underpin professional autonomy, continue to circumscribe and define the powers of the vice-chancellor; there is little evidence of broadening recruitment patterns, and those appointed to the post of vice-chancellor continue to come from similar, predominantly academic backgrounds."(Bargh et al., 2000)

An underlying reason for this is that, despite an increased emphasis on general leadership skills and managerial competence, governing bodies largely continue to hold the view that universities have to be run by academics or those with academic backgrounds, because of the distinctiveness of universities as institutions. Thus, managerial expertise is seen as additional to a strong academic track record rather than the driving consideration in an appointment (Bargh et al., 2000).

Table 3.4 Appointment of leaders of higher education institutions

	Process for election or appointment	Government has to approve?	Typically appointed for how many years?	Renewable position?
	Countries where leaders are usually ELECTED by:			
Finland	Academic staff and heads of separate institutes	No	5	Yes
France	Board or Council	No	5	No
Japan (national)	Academic staff	Yes	4	Varies
Korea (national)	All full-time faculty members	Yes	4	Varies
Switzerland	Senate or ad hoc committee	Yes, mostly	5	Yes
Turkey	All full-time faculty members	Yes	4	Yes
	Countries where leaders are usually APPOINTED by:			
Australia	University Council (majority usually external)	No	5-7	Yes
Ireland	Governing Body (approximately 50% external)	No	10	No
Netherlands	Supervisory Board: 5 external members appointed by Minister	No	4	Yes
Sweden	Government, on recommendation of mainly external Governing Board, which first consults students and employers	Yes	6	Yes, for two periods of 3 years
United Kingdom	Governing Body, of which the majority are external members	No	7	Yes
United States (public)	State government-appointed Regents or Coordinating Boards on the recommendation of Search Committee	No	Varies	Varies
	Countries where reforms have been implemented in 2003:			
Austria	Formerly elected by University Assembly comprising professors (25%), assistant professors (25%), other staff (25%), and students (25%) from the candidates proposed by Senate From 2003, appointed by University Council made up of external members, from a shortlist of three candidates nominated by Senate	No	4	Yes
Denmark	Until July 2003, elected by: academic staff (50%); other staff (25%); and students (25%) From July 2003, appointed by a Board with a majority of external members	No	4	Yes
Norway	Formerly elected by academic and other staff, with some role for students From 2003, an Executive Board with strengthened external representation may propose to the Minister that it appoints the Rector	No	3-4	Yes

Source: Survey of university governance among member institutions of the OECD's Institutional Management in Higher Education (IMHE) programme, conducted by IMHE in 2003. Note 1 to Table 3.1 outlines the scope and limitations of the survey.

7. CONCLUSIONS

Higher education in many OECD countries can still be viewed primarily as a part of the public sector. Governments have a predominant role, either directly providing (as in France) or purchasing or ordering services (as in Sweden). This is true even in countries like the United States where universities have a long history of being entrepreneurial and seeking funds from a variety of sources: the typical four-year college is still largely funded and regulated by state authorities.

Yet markets and competition are increasingly shaping higher education. In some countries (*e.g.* the United Kingdom), this has happened predominantly through competition among public institutions; in others (such as Hungary), through competition between public and private institutions. Increasingly, competition for students and academic staff is taking on an international dimension.

In this context, higher education is moving towards a new system of governance, where the power of markets and the power of the State combine in new ways. Government is generally withdrawing from direct management of institutions, yet at the same time introducing new forms of control and influence, based largely on holding institutions accountable for performance via powerful enforcement mechanisms including funding and quality recognition. Institutions that can no longer take their continued existence for granted are having to work hard both to meet the criteria embedded in funding and regulatory regimes and at the same time to strengthen their position in the marketplace. In the latter task as in the former, institutions cannot afford to stand still. The market for students is both expanding and changing, while competition from a much wider range of providers becomes more intense.

It is within this more demanding environment that the internal governance of higher education institutions is being reassessed. Such institutions need to be able to develop clear organisational strategies backed by decisive and co-ordinated implementation if they are to survive and thrive. What makes the challenge for their leaders if anything more demanding than for a private company is the inherent nature of a university's mission, as first and foremost a generator of knowledge and a community of learners. Effective leadership must take that community with it; university leadership will fail if it leaves "academic" interests behind. The governance of higher education in the 21st century needs to develop a fusion of academic mission and executive capacity, rather than substitute one for the other.

A similar balancing act will be required of governments. Government retains a strong interest in, and a complex range of objectives for, higher education. It will need to regulate the sector, to adopt policies that promote national objectives, to provide incentives to stimulate appropriate improvements by providers, to mobilise from taxpayers the resources needed to meet public goals for higher education, and to ensure equality of opportunity and equity in access. Yet in doing all this, government will need to take care not to replace one potentially counter-productive form of control over higher education with another. The art of policy making will in future involve ensuring that public goals are met in higher education through influence rather than direction.

References

AUSTRIA, FEDERAL MINISTRY OF EDUCATION, SCIENCE AND CULTURE (2002), *University Organisation and Studies Act (Universities Act 2002)*, www.bmbwk.gv.at/medien/8019_ug02_engl.pdf

BARGH, C., BOCOCK, J., SCOTT, P. and **SMITH, D.** (2000), *University Leadership: The Role of the Chief Executive*, Society for Research into Higher Education and Open University Press, London.

BENES, J. and **SEBKOVA, H.** (2002), "Changes and innovations in the governance of the higher education system in the Czech Republic", paper presented to the 16th OECD/IMHE General Conference, September, Paris.

BIFFL, G. and **ISAAC, J.** (2002), "Should higher education students pay tuition fees?", European Journal of Education, Vol. 37, No. 4.

BRAUN, D. and **MERRIEN, F.** (eds.) (1999), *Towards a New Model of Governance for Universities? A Comparative View*, Jessica Kingsley, London.

BRENNAN, J. and **SHAH, T.** (2000), *Managing Quality in Higher Education: An International Perspective on Institutional Assessment and Change*, Society for Research into Higher Education and Open University Press, London.

DE BOER, H. (2000), "Institutional governance: consequences of changed relationships between government and university", paper presented to an OECD/IMHE seminar, Tokyo, 2000.

EURYDICE (2000), *Two Decades of Reform in Higher Education in Europe: 1980 Onwards*, Brussels.

HIGHER EDUCATION FUNDING COUNCIL FOR ENGLAND (2002), *Funding Higher Education in England: How the HEFCE Allocates its Funds*, www.hefce.ac.uk/research/rfund02.htm

HOLTTA, S. and **REKILA, E.** (2002), "Ministerial steering and institutional responses: recent developments for the Finnish higher education system", paper presented to the 16th OECD/IMHE General Conference, September, Paris.

INSTITUTIONAL MANAGEMENT IN HIGHER EDUCATION (IMHE, OECD) and HIGHER EDUCATION FUNDING COUNCIL FOR ENGLAND (HEFCE) (forthcoming), *International Comparative Higher Education Financial Management Project: National Reports*, Paris.

INTERNATIONAL NETWORK FOR QUALITY ASSURANCE AGENCIES IN HIGHER EDUCATION (INQAAHE) (2001), *On-line Survey on Quality Assurance Agencies in Higher Education*, www.inqaahe.nl/public/questionnaires

McDANIEL, O. (1997), "Alternatives to government interference in higher education", Higher Education Management, Vol. 9, No. 2, pp. 115-133.

NEAVE, G. (2001), "Governance, change and the universities", in W. Hirsch and L. Weber (eds.), *Governance in Higher Education: the University in a State of Flux*, Economica, Paris.

NORWAY, MINISTRY OF EDUCATION AND RESEARCH (2003), *The Quality Reform: A Reform In Norwegian Higher Education*, Oslo.

OECD (2002), "The growth of cross-border education", Education Policy Analysis 2002, pp. 89-115, Paris.

OECD (2003a), *Education at a Glance: OECD Indicators 2003*, Paris.

OECD (2003b), *Reviews of National Policies for Education – Tertiary Education in Switzerland*, Paris.

SPORN, B. (2002), "World class reform of universities in Austria", International Higher Education, No. 29 (Fall), pp. 18-19.

VAUGHN, D.L. (2001), *Status on Research Funding at the University of Missouri*, Office of Planning and Budget, University of Missouri, St Louis.

APPENDIX: Country details on aspects of university autonomy

This Appendix elaborates the summary provided in Table 3.1. The numbers in parentheses refer to the columns in Table 3.1 that cover different aspects of autonomy.

Australia	(2) State governments set limits and must approve borrowings. (6) Since 1994 university staff salaries have been determined through an enterprise bargaining process in which salary increases are required to be productivity-related. (7) Universities are able to set the standards for entry into different courses within the constraints of an overall profile negotiated with government. (8) Fees for international and domestic students are subject to government guidelines.
Austria	(1) The buildings are owned by an outsourced institution, Federal Real Estate Association (*Bundes-Immobilien-Gesellschaft*: BIG). Full autonomy concerning equipment. (2) From 2004, however, the Universities Act 2002 will authorise institutions to borrow funds. (5) All newly appointed academic staff after the Universities Act 2002 are to be employed by the university on the basis of private contracts: full autonomy for institutions within legal norms. (6) The salaries for newly appointed academic staff after the Universities Act 2002 will also be negotiated between the newly founded "Austrian universities association" and the unions. The legal status of the "Old" staff will not be changed.
Denmark	(1) Universities hire buildings from a state agency and are free to rent buildings from other providers. From July 2003, a new act permits universities to obtain permission to own their buildings. There is full autonomy regarding ownership of equipment. (4) Although the establishment of a new programme needs to be approved by the ministry, in practice institutions have considerable scope for determining academic structures and course content. (6) Formally there is no constraint on salaries, but in practice institutions offer salaries which exceed the collectively bargained rates by no more than 10%. (8) Institutions can charge tuition fees for part-time students and open university programme only.
Finland	(4) Study fields require a government decree, but this is expected to be changed soon to give institutions more autonomy. (7) Institutions can determine their entrance capacity provided that the degree targets agreed with the Ministry of Education will be reached.
Ireland	(2) Universities have autonomy to borrow subject to a framework agreed between the universities and the funding agency, the Higher Education Authority. In practice, this means they can borrow freely provided the transaction is on a self-funding basis (*e.g.* for student housing) and may borrow for other purposes, provided that the financing costs (including repayment) based on a ten-year repayment period, do not exceed 4% of income, defined as total core teaching income (state grant, student fees and sundry income) plus research income. (6) Universities can decide the salaries of their personnel subject to approval of Minister for Education and Science and Minister for Finance. (8) Universities have the legal right to determine fees but, since the State pays most of the undergraduate fees, consultation take place.
Japan (national/public)	(4) Institutions have autonomy in the establishment of a new programme within existing structures and course contents only. (5) Formal decision regarding employment of academic staff is taken by the government, but actual consideration of these decisions is made by the university concerned. See Box 3.1 for forthcoming changes introduced by the National University Corporation Law in Japan.
Korea (national/public)	(4) Institutions have autonomy in the establishment of a new programme within existing structures and course content only. (5) The positions funded by sources other than state are not subject to state position control, all requirements and benefits of the state civil service. In employing academic staff, formal decision is taken by the government, but actual consideration of these decisions is made by the university concerned. (7) The number of students in the institutions located in Seoul should be approved by the government. This restriction is also applied to private universities.
Mexico	(2) Institutions can borrow funds on the condition that the Board of Trustees approve. (6) Institutions can determine the salaries of their staff provided that they obtain the funds necessary for such expenditure in addition to those provided by government. (8) In practice, the level of tuition fees is low.
Netherlands	(4) The establishment of a new programme of study must be approved by the Netherlands Accreditation Organisation (NAO) if degrees are to be awarded, and by the Ministry of Education for funding. (6) Universities can decide the salaries of their personnel if broadly consistent with agreements at other universities. (8) Since 1996 universities have been able to determine their own tuition fees for part-time courses and those that alternate with work experience (sandwich courses). Universities of Professional Education (HBOs), however, generally keep tuition fees at the minimum rates set by the government.

(continued on next page)

Norway	(1) All university property is owned by the State. Universities have some limited authority concerning buildings, but full autonomy concerning equipment. (6) Institutions can decide salaries of their staff provided they fall within guidelines set by the government.
Poland	(6) Institutions can decide staff salaries provided they do not exceed state-formulated limits. (8) Institutions can decide the level of tuition fees only for studies other than full-time day programmes, which are free.
Sweden	(1) The ownership of assets other than buildings is devolved to institutions. The buildings are normally rented by Academiska Hus AB, a state-owned enterprise. However, institutions are free to choose who to rent from and to decide the share of their budget for buildings. (2) Institutions can borrow from the Swedish National Debt Office. The government sets the maximum amount of loans and credits allowable. Borrowing from private financers is not allowed. (7) Institutions can determine their entrance capacity provided that institutional tasks laid down by the budget document are fulfilled.
Turkey	(4) Institutions can determine their academic structure provided the Higher Education Council approves. (5) Institutions can employ their staff as long as positions are open. (7) Institutions can determine their own entrance capacity for graduate school only.
United Kingdom	(2) Institutions can borrow funds provided they do not exceed borrowing thresholds set by the Funding Councils. (7) Institutions can determine their entrance capacity provided they achieve their contracted number of students across broad subject categories. (8) Tuition fees are subject to government ceilings.

Source: Survey of university governance among member institutions of the OECD's Institutional Management in Higher Education (IMHE) programme, conducted by IMHE in 2003. See Table 3.1, Note 1.

chapter 4
STRATEGIES FOR SUSTAINABLE INVESTMENT IN ADULT LIFELONG LEARNING

Summary 80

1. INTRODUCTION 81

2. ADULT LEARNING: THE WEAK LINK IN THE LIFELONG LEARNING FRAMEWORK 81

3. EVALUATING ECONOMIC SUSTAINABILITY 84
    3.1 Results of the analysis 88
    3.2 The impact of reduced study time due to accreditation of prior learning 90
    3.3 Policy lessons for enhancing economic sustainability 91

4. IMPROVING FINANCIAL SUSTAINABILITY 92
    4.1 Overview of past approaches 92
    4.2 Strategies for co-financing lifelong learning..93
    4.3 Results and lessons to date 97

5. CONCLUSIONS AND POLICY PRIORITIES 98

References 99

Data for the Figure 101

CHAPTER 4

STRATEGIES FOR SUSTAINABLE INVESTMENT IN ADULT LIFELONG LEARNING

SUMMARY

Lifelong learning is a core strategy for moving to a knowledge society, and ensuring that the benefits are equitably distributed. However, adult learning is the weak link in the lifelong learning framework. Although the benefits of adult learning cannot be expressed in financial terms alone, economic considerations are important. If individuals, enterprises and governments are to invest more in adult learning, it must be "economically sustainable" (projected benefits must be sufficient to offset the costs) and "financially sustainable" (there must be a means of paying today for benefits that may arrive well into the future). While investment in young people's education is highly sustainable in both senses, this is less true for adult learning.

This chapter first sheds light on the economic sustainability of adult learning by making illustrative calculations about rates of return from mid-life study. Its findings suggest that, under prevailing policy, the economic returns provide only modest incentives for individuals – particularly adults in employment – to undertake more lifelong learning. Intervention is needed to ease the burden of foregone earnings and to shorten study periods by giving adult learners credit for what they already know.

The financial sustainability of adult learning hinges on mechanisms to share costs among individuals, government and employers. Governments should cover costs for the least advantaged, and create the means for other parties to share costs. The chapter explores recent initiatives in 10 OECD countries that aim to make such "co-financing" a reality. They have shown promise, although it has proven difficult to reach those disadvantaged groups who badly need new learning opportunities. Nevertheless, the wide range of initiatives now underway provides insights on what might work for individuals and enterprises.

CHAPTER 4

STRATEGIES FOR SUSTAINABLE INVESTMENT
IN ADULT LIFELONG LEARNING

1. INTRODUCTION[1]

Education systems continued to expand in the 1990s, buoyed by the centrality of learning in today's knowledge societies. A wider section of the population than ever before is accessing education outside the compulsory school years: upper secondary education has become the norm, and increasing proportions of young people are participating in early childhood and tertiary education. Yet, progress towards widening access to ongoing education and training for adults has been more limited, and this has caused concern in OECD countries committed to an ideal of "lifelong learning".

An important driver of the expansion of initial education has been growth in awareness of individual and social benefits or returns to education, boosted by greater measurement of these returns. In general such measurements have estimated the lifetime benefits of completing a particular stage of education during one's youth – with benefits ranging from the individual earnings payoff of obtaining a university degree to the social gains from a child participating in a pre-primary programme. This improved understanding has contributed both to the willingness of the public sector to contribute to the cost of expansion (recognising the wider social benefits of education) and the willingness of individuals and families to share costs (recognising the private benefits of education).

Far harder to measure are the consequences of adult lifelong learning: the more varied, and less standardised ways in which people invest in learning after the end of initial education – whether via "second chance" education in later life, topping up of skills, or renewing qualifications in a changing world. Yet in order to make adult learning *economically sustainable*, it must visibly generate sufficient returns to offset its cost. The existence of such economic benefits is necessary, but not sufficient, to guarantee that the investment will be made. It also needs to be *financially sustainable*: the learning needs to be able to be paid for at the time it takes place, although the benefits may not arise until some time in the future.

This chapter looks at the factors that constrain the economic and financial sustainability of adult learning, and at policy options that might reduce those constraints. In doing so it suggests new ways of measuring economic sustainability, illustrating through simulations the payoffs that can be expected in different circumstances. This analysis aims to start filling a gap in understanding, which potentially constrains investment in lifelong learning, and has important implications for policy. Yet it is only a starting point in addressing sustainability, and the chapter also raises questions for future research.

Section 2 sets the scene by considering barriers to the spread of adult learning and how these are linked to difficulties in making learning throughout life economically and financially sustainable. Section 3 then looks specifically at how economic sustainability can be evaluated, bringing in the new analyses, while Section 4 considers the determinants of financial sustainability, and recent initiatives in cost sharing. Section 5 draws the main implications together.

2. ADULT LEARNING: THE WEAK LINK IN THE LIFELONG LEARNING FRAMEWORK

By the mid-1990s it was evident that, although formal education systems were expanding to help meet demand for *initial* education, they were not able to ensure lifelong learning for all. One important gap concerned adequate provision for young children; in the past few years, this area has been strengthened considerably (see OECD, 2001a). Another shortfall concerned adults: in particular, those with low levels of initial qualifications not only faced increasing difficulty in finding and holding employment, but they were having difficulty in gaining effective access to opportunities for improving their knowledge and skills. This fundamental difficulty persists (OECD and U.S. Department of Education, 1997; OECD, 2003a).

---

1. This chapter draws on an OECD working paper prepared with support from the Swiss Federal authorities. For further details see Wurzburg and De Sousa (2002).

CHAPTER 4

STRATEGIES FOR SUSTAINABLE INVESTMENT
IN ADULT LIFELONG LEARNING

> **Lifelong learning, initial education, adult learning – some distinctions**
>
> This chapter uses *initial education* to refer to primary, secondary and tertiary education carried out as a more or less continuous sequence by children and young adults. *Adult lifelong learning* on the other hand refers to education and training that occurs subsequently. This may be a way of gaining the main formal secondary and tertiary qualifications that were not obtained initially ("second chance" education), or may involve various other forms of study, formal or informal, which may or may not lead to a variety of qualifications. *Lifelong learning* includes early childhood education, initial education and adult learning; it describes not only these stages in combination but also an overall approach to learning that spans all three.

Many barriers have contributed to the limited degree to which adults in general and disadvantaged adults in particular participate in learning. Teaching methods are not always appropriate, and individuals may lack accessible and supportive services needed to balance work, family and learning (OECD, 2003a). This chapter focuses on a particularly critical barrier, that of resources, which involves limits on time and money. The shift to a paradigm of lifelong learning poses a more complex resource challenge than earlier fundamental changes such as the introduction of universal secondary education. Lifelong learning changes a number of parameters in ways that are not clearcut: who the learners are; the scale, nature, timing, and duration of learning; what is learned; and where. The fact that this has major cost implications is clear; by how much is less clear. While the OECD has illustrated the cost to countries of building a sound basis for lifelong learning (OECD, 2000), this has been largely confined to initial education for young people. As yet, the resources needed for more extensive adult learning have not been systematically analysed. OECD countries face critical questions about how to achieve and sustain the increased levels of investment needed to ensure that opportunities are available to all those who seek them, and to ensure that society is investing at economically efficient levels.

The vast human capital literature that has grown over the past few decades has centred on evaluating the *economic sustainability* of investment in various forms of education and training (*i.e.* its capacity to generate sufficient returns to offset its cost). Concentrating mainly on outcomes in adulthood from various stages of initial educational attainment, it has compared the benefits to individuals and society to the direct costs of provision and indirect costs in terms of foregone earnings and production. The costs and benefits of education investments have been measured from the perspective of individuals (private internal rates of return), governments (fiscal rates of return), and society at large (social rates of return),[2] as well as from the perspective of companies.[3]

The *financial sustainability* of such investments is another matter. This refers to the capacity to pay today for an investment for which the economic benefits may not eventuate until well into the future. This is conditional not just on economic factors but on particular circumstances influencing the current ability or willingness to pay. In the case of learning, this includes the context in which public contributions are made. Thus, for example, the financial sustainability of investment in primary and secondary education is influenced by political support for education spending, by the general fiscal health of public finances, and by the nature and coherence of funding sources (such as funding from a single level or multiple levels of government). Financial sustainability for adult learning may depend, in addition, on the ability of individuals and/or employers to assume at least part of the financial burden of direct education costs and/or foregone earnings. For individuals, this ability may be influenced by the availability of loans on reasonable terms, or tax credits for study costs. For employers it may be influenced by the extent to which they can reduce the risks associated with such investment, or demonstrate that it generates a relatively high return.

---

2. For example, OECD (1998a, 2002a); Mellander and Skedinger (1999); and Blöndal et al. (2002).

3. For example, Otterstein et al. (1999); and Bassi et al. (2000).

CHAPTER 4

STRATEGIES FOR SUSTAINABLE INVESTMENT IN ADULT LIFELONG LEARNING

Lifelong learning entails more than just extending provision of standardised forms of education to a wider range of age-groups. It serves a spectrum of objectives, ranging from preparing to learn at school (for pre-school children), to updating work-related competencies for current jobs, to upgrading qualifications and competencies for different jobs, to personal development, and learning as a leisure activity. It puts the learner at the centre of initiating learning, setting objectives and evaluating outcomes, especially in adulthood, rather than just using public priorities to shape provision. Moreover, it does not see discrete learning stages in isolation but takes a systemic view of relationships between different types of learning over the course of people's lives (OECD, 2001*b*; OECD, 2001*c*).

These features have critical consequences for the economic and financial sustainability of investments in adult lifelong learning. In particular:

- The learning process in adulthood is more *demand driven and individualised*. In contrast to a system defined by formal education and training stages based on universal or mass participation, lifelong learning is conceived as a process that facilitates acquisition of a virtually infinite possible range of skills and competencies for individuals with different starting and finishing points. This heterogeneity implies, in turn, greater reliance on smoothly functioning markets for education, training and learning opportunities, in which barriers to multiple suppliers are low, and individuals have incentives to express demand. The latter condition relies on credible and visible signals of educational outcomes, so that students can predict with greater certainty that a learning episode will provide an economic or other benefit. Another important form of certification is credit for prior learning, for adults who wish to re-enter formal education without either the psychological discouragement of having to duplicate what they already know, or the weakening of economic incentives caused by an extended duration of study.

- Insofar as a lifelong learning framework *shifts the timing of learning activities into adulthood*, there is a high likelihood that the private returns will increase relative to the social returns. Those private returns include higher wages and a higher probability of employment for individuals, and increased productivity and profitability for enterprises. Thus, while high levels of social returns justify public funding of education and training at least through the level of upper secondary education, the same cannot necessarily be said for learning by working-age adults. This suggests that, at least in the case of individuals who are not seriously at risk in labour markets (for whom there may be clear social benefit arguments for public funding of learning), individuals and employers should assume a major part of the burden of financing adult learning.

- Financial and economic sustainability are made more difficult by the *high cost of study* for adults of working age, including foregone earnings during study time, the direct costs of study, and competing priorities that are associated with family responsibilities, particularly for adults on low incomes. Older adults tend to be more reluctant to cover such costs through loans because of their shorter earning horizon. Student financial support schemes tend to be focused on the needs of younger persons, particularly with regard to living expenses.[4]

Combining these factors, it is clear that greater obstacles impede the financial and economic sustainability of learning in the adult years than at younger ages in the life cycle. Is adult learning an economically and financially sustainable investment? It would appear that frequently it is not *in the context of prevailing policy and existing institutional arrangements*.[5]

Can policy enhance the economic and financial sustainability of investing in lifelong learning for adults and, if so, how? The next two sections present the results of recent work that provides a basis for beginning to answer these questions.

---

4. OECD (2002*b*) discusses the difficulties of adapting student support schemes to the needs of adult learners.

5. Cohn and Addison (1998) analyse a considerable body of international evidence on returns to, among other things, vocational and occupational training. Their analysis suggests that the returns in most cases are low.

3. EVALUATING ECONOMIC SUSTAINABILITY

The economic sustainability of investment in the education of young people is well established (OECD, 2002a). But what about the economic sustainability of investment in adult learning; does that investment pay for itself in the same way as the investment in initial education? In the case of formal education, this raises the issue of whether middle-aged adults who upgrade qualifications gain such substantial payoffs, relative to the cost, as younger people. In the case of adults who simply want to update prior qualifications or acquire particular competencies (*e.g.* learning a foreign language or new computer skills), the cost may be less but are the returns sufficient to pay for it?

Economic sustainability can be summarised by the *internal rate of return* of an investment – the annual rate of payoff when comparing future benefits to

---

Box 4.1 Internal rates of return

Internal rates of return compare economic benefits and costs, in terms of an annual percentage return to an investment. The higher the internal rate of return for a given investment, the stronger the incentive to invest, and to compete for capital resources with other possible investments.

The internal rate of return is calculated as the "discount" rate (the rate of trade-off between the value of money now and of money next year) that would be required to make the present value of the benefits equal to that of the costs associated with the investment. It is necessary to express income and costs in present value terms since the value of additional income anticipated in say 10 years is less than the value of the same amount of money forgone today. In analysing education investments (*e.g.* in a university degree), the estimated rate of return is calculated by finding the rate of discount that equates (i) the present value of an estimated future stream of *additional* income (compared to having an upper secondary qualification, in the case of investing in a university degree) over a lifetime to (ii) the present value of the *additional* cost of studying (including foregone earnings).

The relative attractiveness of investments depends on who is paying and who benefits. In this chapter rates of return were calculated from two perspectives: individuals (private rate of return); and governments (fiscal rate of return). For individuals the additional income from a given level of education was estimated as the difference in average *net* income (*i.e.* gross income minus income tax and social service contributions) between people with different levels of education in the population aged 15-64. The additional costs of studying for a qualification were estimated from (i) the average private contribution to total education spending at the level concerned, and (ii) average net foregone earnings (*i.e.* gross income minus income tax and social service contributions for people with the lower level of education).

For governments, the additional income from a given level of education was estimated as the average difference in income tax and employee social service contributions paid by people with different levels of education attainment, minus the average level of social transfers (*e.g.* unemployment, family and retirement benefits) paid by governments to people with different levels of educational attainment. The additional costs to government were estimated as the public contribution to total education spending at the level concerned and lost tax revenue on earnings foregone over the duration of study.

Further details on the methodology and data used in this chapter are provided in OECD (1998a). The uses and limitations of rates of return are discussed in more detail in OECD (1998b and 2002a).

costs (see Box 4.1). The higher the internal rate of return for investment in lifelong learning, the stronger the economic incentive to invest. If the rate of return is high compared to other possible investments, such investment is more likely to compete effectively for resources.

Which costs and benefits can be taken into account? Ideally, these should include non-economic costs and benefits (*e.g.* the enjoyment of learning), although in practice it is economic ones that are most readily quantified. Measurable costs and benefits include:

Costs	Benefits
To individuals	
Direct: fees, transportation, instructional supplies	Higher wages, higher chances of employment, greater job mobility
Indirect: foregone earnings, foregone leisure	
To employers	
Direct: as above where paid directly by employer	Increased productivity not fully covered by higher wages
Indirect: foregone production during training	Enhanced employee flexibility
To governments	
Financing of courses; transfer payments to individuals when studying/training	Higher tax revenues; general economic benefits of a more flexible, productive workforce

However, the components that determine whether education investments will be economically sustainable can in practice be hard to evaluate. This is particularly true in making judgements in public policy about the sustainability of lifelong learning. This concept embraces a wide scope of learning activities, with widely different types of costs and benefits. Moreover, returns to lifelong learning look different from different perspectives, be they the perspective of the individual, the employer, the public purse or society at large.

Yet whatever difficulties and consequent imperfections in evaluating economic sustainability, political commitments to facilitate lifelong learning, with consequent resource implications, make it important to find ways of doing so. The following analysis attempts an illustrative evaluation of this type, by simulating internal rates of return under scenarios that embody core concerns of lifelong policies. Specifically, this simulation has calculated rates of return using:

- *Two cases* of hypothetical individuals. Both are 40-year-olds stopping work and returning to formal education to acquire the next highest level of qualification. The first case is someone with only lower secondary education getting an upper secondary diploma; the second is someone with upper secondary education who obtains a university-level first degree.

- *Benefits* calculated from the average difference in earnings between people with the original and the acquired qualification level,[6] assuming that those acquiring education later in life would eventually catch up with the pay of those getting it earlier.

- *Costs* comprising: direct costs in terms of the actual cost of study reported by national authorities; plus indirect costs (income foregone) calculated from age-earnings profiles, and also taking account of changes in transfer payments.

- *Two perspectives*: of individuals (to calculate "private internal rates of return") and of public authorities (for "fiscal internal rates of return"). The perspectives of enterprises which are also important are excluded for the sake of keeping the stylised analysis reasonably simple and because many of

---

6. The analysis focuses on adults acquiring formal educational qualifications since such data are more readily available, and at present there are not fully developed institutional arrangements that would allow individuals to reap financial rewards for "intermediate" levels of attainment or qualifications acquired through non-formal learning (see Colardyn, 2002, pp. 31-33).

the important issues arising in enterprise investment in training are dealt with in other analyses.[7] Nevertheless, the enterprise perspective is considered below in the policy discussion.

The analysis based on these calculations was not meant to estimate actual returns but rather explore the impact on returns of factors – such as costs – that can be influenced by policy. In doing so it explores the *potential* for policy initiatives to make a difference. It also allows one to identify where certain investments do *not* bring sufficient returns to make them economically sustainable under present policy and institutional arrangements. The approach uses the estimates to identify the factors that "drive" internal rates of return: factors that lower economic costs, raise economic benefits, and reduce the cost of capital. It seeks to identify effective ways of fulfilling the economic and social goals of lifting adult participation in learning, *and* influencing positively future rates of return.

At the same time, several limitations of the analysis must be recognised:

- The stylised cases used, of adults in mid-career leaving work to study full-time to obtain a higher qualification, are rarely seen in practice at present. Nevertheless, labour market analysis pointing to the need for extended periods of requalification and training rather than reliance solely on initial education shows that major forms of study in mid-working life are desirable even if not the current prevailing pattern. Moreover, the results of the stylised cases provide a basis against which to evaluate other approaches, such as part-time study outside working hours, that may involve foregoing little income but greater amounts of leisure time, which is harder to value.

- The analysis assumes in some of the scenarios that the duration of study for adults can be reduced by accreditation for prior learning gained through working experience. In practice, while institutions in some countries make such provision, there is no systematic data on the amount, its costs or impact. Thus the analysis shows the *potential* of a particular practice rather than the extent to which it presently occurs.

- The analysis makes certain assumptions about the trajectory of the earnings of people in their early 40s who have just progressed from a lower to a higher qualification level; these are "guesstimates" rather than being based directly on evidence, which is sparse, although there are some indicative data for Sweden, the United Kingdom[8] and Canada (see Box 4.2). The assumptions are: (i) that such people start by earning more than those people with the lower qualification but less than those who acquired the higher one in initial education in their early 20s; and (ii) that their earnings converge with those of the latter in 10 years after gaining the higher qualification.

- The calculations are based on a data set from 1995, which provides information for a range of countries and has been used in earlier OECD analyses of the internal rates of return to formal education (OECD, 1998*a* and 1998*b*).[9] Although it is unlikely that the relationships revealed by these data have changed much in the intervening period, it would be desirable to repeat the analyses with more up-to-date data.

---

7. The calculation of returns to enterprises from financing education and training is not straightforward. The potential payoff for firms can take the form of short- and long-term profitability, as well as market capitalisation (Bassi *et al.*, 2000). Furthermore, the costs facing firms are complex and it can be difficult to separate the costs of education and training (OECD, 2003*b*).

8. One study that used 50 years of longitudinal data for a cohort of Swedish men found that the correlation between earnings and initial education declined with age, while the correlation between earnings and participation in adult education rose to a peak at age 43 before declining, though more slowly than for initial education (Tuijnman, 1989). The correlation between participation in adult education and occupational status was stronger, increased steadily, and by age 56 nearly equalled that of initial education. The general conclusion was that adult learning had a strong influence on occupational status and earnings. Jenkins *et al.* (2002) used longitudinal data from the United Kingdom to analyse the impact of obtaining a qualification between the ages of 33 and 42. They found that individuals with no qualifications in 1991 who later obtained a qualification were earning higher wages by 2000 than those who had not engaged in study during the period. There were also some positive wage effects for those who already had qualifications and who obtained a higher qualification during the period, although the results were more mixed. One of the strongest results was that "learning leads to learning": studying for a qualification increased the probability of the individual undertaking more learning.

9. Data were analysed for seven countries: Australia; Canada; Denmark; France; Norway; Sweden; and the United States. Details on the data and methodology are provided in OECD (1998*a*, Annex 3).

CHAPTER 4

STRATEGIES FOR SUSTAINABLE INVESTMENT
IN ADULT LIFELONG LEARNING

Box 4.2 **What actually happens to the earnings of adult learners? Evidence from Canada**

The Canadian Survey of Labour and Income Dynamics (SLID) is a panel survey that tracks individuals for up to six years. Because SLID collects extensive information on an annual basis from the same individuals it enables more detailed analysis of the effect of changes in qualifications than is normally provided by cross-section data at a single point in time. Specifically, the OECD Secretariat used SLID data to examine the earnings of individuals, aged 30-49, who acquired a formal education qualification in the middle of a five-year interval (*i.e.* those obtaining a qualification in the third of the five years, so that "before and after" earnings could be analysed). The qualifications included a college certificate or a university degree. (Qualification at upper secondary level was also considered but there were too few cases to analyse.) The earnings profiles of such individuals were then compared with those of similar age who had not upgraded their qualifications. Figure 4.1 shows the results for the period 1993-98.

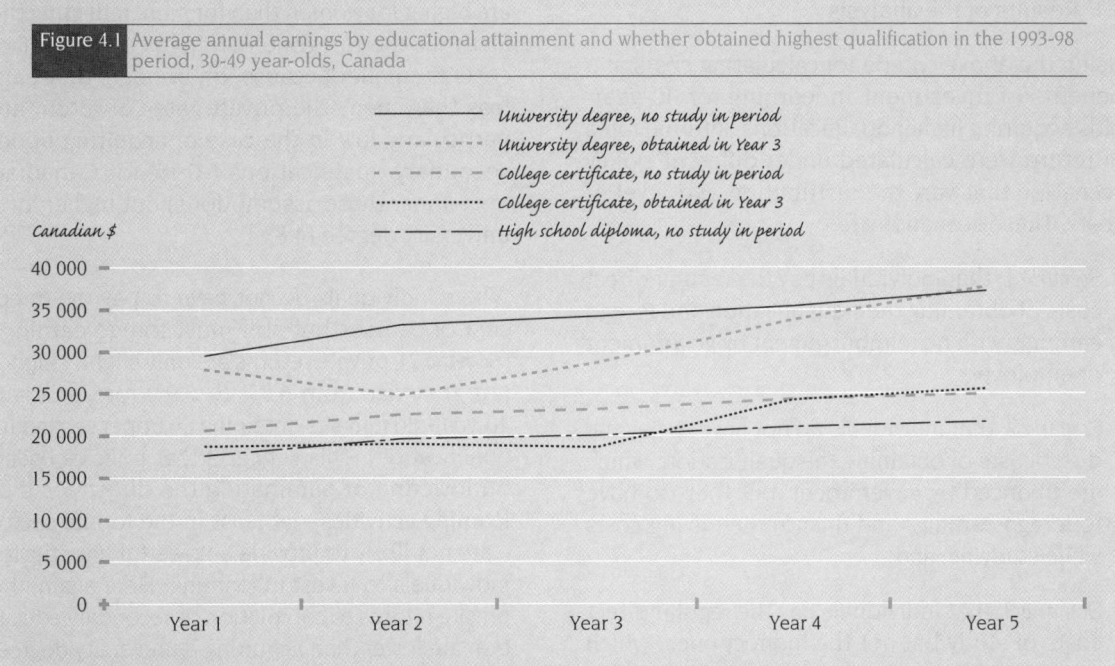

Figure 4.1 Average annual earnings by educational attainment and whether obtained highest qualification in the 1993-98 period, 30-49 year-olds, Canada

Source: OECD Secretariat analysis of data from the Canadian Survey of Labour and Income Dynamics, 1993-98 panel.
Data for Figure 4.1, p. 101.

The findings indicate that those who upgraded their qualifications in Year 3 of the 5-year period experienced rapid earnings growth over the next two years: by 32% for those obtaining a university degree; and 37% for a college certificate. By contrast, the three groups shown in Figure 4.1 who did not upgrade their qualifications experienced growth of only 8-9% over those two years. Those 30-49 year-olds who obtained a higher qualification in Year 3 in fact only took two years to catch up with the average earnings of those who already held that level of qualification. The upward trajectory of earnings for those with upgraded qualifications is very steep which indicates that the assumptions about earnings gains that underlie the analysis in this chapter may be conservative, and that the estimated returns may underestimate the actual returns for the various scenarios.

(*continued on next page*)

> However, these findings are far from definitive. Only 1% of the samples did in fact upgrade their qualifications to college or university level over the five-year period, so the results are subject to caveats about small and possibly unrepresentative numbers. First and foremost is the issue of whether all things are indeed equal: are those who obtained upgraded qualifications otherwise the same as those who did not? Or are there unobserved characteristics of learners (higher degree of motivation, stronger employer support and so on) that play a role in the decision to learn or not learn, and which are also an influence on earnings? As a possible pointer to this explanation, those who upgraded to a university degree in Year 3 already had relatively high earnings (although those who upgraded to a college certificate did not). Nevertheless, when combined with the Swedish longitudinal analyses by Tuijnman (1989), and the United Kingdom analyses by Jenkins *et al.* (2002), these Canadian results suggest that adult learning can, indeed, have a strong influence on occupational status and earnings.

3.1 Results of the analysis

Using the above criteria for calculating costs and benefits of investment in learning for 40-year-olds acquiring higher qualifications, internal rates of return were calculated under different policy scenarios that vary the distribution and level of costs. These scenarios are:

- *Scenario* 1: that individuals pay the regular direct costs of obtaining their qualification and forego earnings with no reimbursement by government or employer;

- *Scenario* 2: that individuals do not have to pay the direct costs of obtaining the qualification, which are financed by government, but they do have to forego earnings and finance their living costs while studying; and

- *Scenario* 3: that individuals pay the regular direct costs of study but not the indirect ones, which are covered by an employer who pays the salary of an employee on leave.

The results of these calculations are summarised in Table 4.1, which shows the private and fiscal rates of return for adults acquiring upper secondary and university-level qualifications. Rates for males and females are shown separately. For the sake of brevity, returns are shown for one country only, Canada, and cases where patterns differ significantly in other countries are noted in the text.[10] The results indicate that:

- With no subsidy either to direct or indirect costs (*Scenario* 1), returns to individuals are low. They are higher for women than for men, reflecting the fact that the foregone earnings component of costs is smaller because, on average, they earn less than men. The private rates of return are particularly low in the case of acquiring upper secondary qualifications (-0.1% for Canadian men under these assumptions) but higher for a university degree (4.8%).

- Where individuals do not have to pay the direct cost of courses but still must forego earnings (*Scenario* 2), private returns are only slightly higher (*e.g.* they rise from 6.5% to 6.9% for Canadian 40-year-old females obtaining an upper secondary qualification). This suggests that policies based on lowering or eliminating the direct costs of learning activities – at least in the formal sector – are not likely to provide a powerful impetus for individuals to invest in learning. Here again, the private returns to completion of secondary education are lower than acquiring a university degree. While returns in the other countries analysed were slightly higher than in Canada, the patterns are the same, mainly well below 10%, with the exceptions being for women in France and the United States for whom they reach 12.5%.

- It is where individuals do not have to forego earnings (*Scenario* 3) that private rates of return are

---

10. The calculations for Canada are included since on most measures the Canadian results are close to the average of the countries concerned, and there is a different, more recent set of data available for Canada (see Box 4.2) that helps to elaborate the discussion. Full results on the countries analysed are in Wurzburg and De Sousa (2002).

CHAPTER 4

STRATEGIES FOR SUSTAINABLE INVESTMENT IN ADULT LIFELONG LEARNING

Table 4.1 **Rates of return to obtaining upper secondary and university degree qualifications: illustrative data for 40-year-olds, Canada**

Scenario	Private internal rate of return (%) Males	Private internal rate of return (%) Females	Fiscal internal rate of return (%) Males	Fiscal internal rate of return (%) Females
Upper secondary qualifications				
1: Individual pays regular direct costs and has no reimbursement for foregone earnings while studying	-0.1	6.5	-0.6	3.1
2: Individual does not pay direct costs (paid by government) but has no reimbursement for foregone earnings while studying	0.1	6.9	-0.8	2.7
3: Individual pays regular direct costs but employer reimburses foregone earnings	7.4	24.5	1.5	3.7
University degree qualifications				
1: Individual pays regular direct costs and has no reimbursement for foregone earnings while studying	4.8	9.9	5.4	6.2
2: Individual does not pay direct costs (paid by government) but has no reimbursement for foregone earnings while studying	5.3	10.8	4.8	5.3
3: Individual pays regular direct costs but employer reimburses foregone earnings	25.9	35.2	8.8	7.8

by far the highest. This is because for 40-year-olds in full-time employment foregone earnings will be more significant than the direct costs of study. Table 4.1 also indicates that the private rates of return under these assumptions are greater for university qualifications than completing secondary education (*e.g.* 35.2% and 24.5% respectively, for Canadian women). Under this scenario the returns for Canada are lower than the returns for other countries. Elsewhere the return for acquiring upper secondary qualifications ranged for males from 17% in France to around 40% in Denmark and the United States, and for females up to about 50% in Denmark and the United States. Returns for acquiring university degrees were everywhere higher still, except in the United States where they were around 20%.

- In all three scenarios, fiscal returns to government are lower than the private returns to individuals. This is true in all the countries analysed except Denmark and Norway, where more compressed wage structures, relatively greater reductions in economic dependency and increased tax revenues all lead to a higher net benefit to the public purse than to private individuals. From a government fiscal perspective, the Canadian results in Table 4.1 show that the returns to university-level education for 40-year-olds are higher than for completing upper secondary education. However, among the other countries there was less consistency in whether acquiring upper secondary or university-level qualifications produced higher fiscal rates of return.

- The higher private returns associated with university study reflect the fact that for individuals, wage differentials associated with progression from upper secondary to university-level qualifications tend to be much higher than from lower secondary to upper secondary (the costs are higher, too, but by a proportionately lower amount). However, in the case of fiscal returns, increased tax revenues accruing from this higher pay are in some cases outweighed by the greater benefit of the raised employment chances and therefore reduced welfare dependency of people acquiring upper secondary qualifications.

3.2 The impact of reduced study time due to accreditation of prior learning

Rates of return for these same scenarios were recalculated assuming that the duration of education was reduced by half from the standard length associated with each qualification level. This is an indicator of the return available if an individual receives academic credit for work experience (accreditation of prior learning or APL), sufficient to halve course study duration – which the analysis assumes to be available to someone with about 20 years' work experience. Whether that figure is appropriate is debatable.[11] Though such credits have a long history, there is scant empirical evidence to show the number of students who are awarded credit for prior learning, the amount awarded, or the cost of the process for assessing prior learning. What evidence there is suggests that, so far, APL is still not widely used.[12] However, around 1-2 years of academic credit for 20 years of work experience does not seem too unreasonable as an assumption, or alternatively as a target for policy.

Table 4.2 records the results of reduced study time through APL. The results show substantial increases on the rates of return reported in Table 4.1. The increases apply both to private and fiscal rates. This reflects the importance of foregone earnings as a component of the costs of adult learning. It also reflects lower direct costs because of shorter course duration, and the fact that shorter courses mean individuals have a longer period over which to enjoy the higher earnings benefits from upgraded qualifications.[13]

Overall, the analysis suggests that:

- In the absence of interventions that reduce direct costs or indirect costs, the incentives for a working adult to invest in lifelong learning are rather weak. Adults who have to take full responsibility for the cost of fees, draw on savings and/or take out loans to cover costs of living, get much lower returns than those that apply for young people undertaking initial education and training, for whom foregone earnings are lower and the earnings horizon after graduation is longer. As Table 4.1 showed, under some circumstances the estimated returns are even negative. This suggests that weak economic incentives are an important factor behind the low rates of adult participation in lifelong learning.

- Incentives for less qualified persons to invest in lifelong learning are weaker than incentives for more qualified persons, since the private returns to upgrading qualifications rise with education level. This helps to explain lower participation rates among less educated groups, with low returns adding to other potential barriers such as inappropriate pedagogy, lack of employer encouragement and poor motivation.

- Fiscal returns – the internal rate of return for government – to investment in adult learning tend to be substantially smaller than the returns for individuals under these assumptions.

- The rates of return for females participating in adult learning under these scenarios are nearly always higher than returns for men (Norway is an exception). The main reason for this is that since women's earnings are lower on average than those of men, women tend to have lower indirect costs of study (foregone earnings).

However, this latter result should be treated with caution. Differential effects on earnings between men and women of acquiring qualifications in midlife could make a difference to their respective rates

---

11. For some adults returning to formal education it may even take longer than usual to complete a given qualification because of their unfamiliarity with the study materials or learning environment.

12. A recent review of the Australian vocational education and training sector indicated that around 4% of students received some recognition of prior learning on enrolment, with the incidence being greater for the highest level qualifications (about 10%) than for lower qualifications (about 2%), and also greater for older students than younger students (Bateman and Knight, 2003). Another Australian study using a different data set reported that around 5% of higher education students and 8% of vocational education and training students received credit for prior learning (Wheelahan et al., 2002).

13. Note, however, that the costs of applying for accreditation for prior learning are not included in the analysis, nor are the other costs of APL schemes.

CHAPTER 4
STRATEGIES FOR SUSTAINABLE INVESTMENT IN ADULT LIFELONG LEARNING

Table 4.2 Rates of return to obtaining upper secondary and university degree qualifications: illustrative data for 40-year-olds, who obtain a 50% reduction in study time through accreditation of prior learning, Canada

Scenario	Private internal rate of return (%) Males	Private internal rate of return (%) Females	Fiscal internal rate of return (%) Males	Fiscal internal rate of return (%) Females
Upper secondary qualifications				
1: Individual pays regular direct costs and has no reimbursement for foregone earnings while studying	2.8	11.1	3.6	9.7
2: Individual does not pay direct costs (paid by government) but has no reimbursement for foregone earnings while studying	3.7	13.6	2.1	7.3
3: Individual pays regular direct costs but employer reimburses foregone earnings	8.1	28.6	5.8	10.5
University degree qualifications				
1: Individual pays regular direct costs and has no reimbursement for foregone earnings while studying	10.6	17.5	12.3	41.7
2: Individual does not pay direct costs (paid by government) but has no reimbursement for foregone earnings while studying	11.1	18.8	11.4	38.2
3: Individual pays regular direct costs but employer reimburses foregone earnings	42.1	64.9	17.1	48.9

of return, and this is not measured here since the earnings data are derived from what people earn with given qualifications acquired in *initial* education. The other calculated returns must also be interpreted with this deficiency in mind, though Box 4.2 suggests that a mid-life qualification, at least in Canada, strongly influences earnings. More generally, the reader is reminded that these results do not take into account the rates of return to employers, nor do they take into account learning that does not lead to a qualification or that takes place in addition to (rather than instead of) employment.

3.3 Policy lessons for enhancing economic sustainability

The preceding analysis attempts to develop tools for evaluating the economic sustainability of adult learning within the lifelong learning framework. It does so by looking at how policy options affecting costs can influence returns, and by observing how returns can differ for different actors. The results offer some initial conclusions that merit further investigation, that help frame a more systematic approach to the formulation of options, and that help target further empirical investigation.

The analyses indicate that internal rates of return are highly sensitive to variations in a set of cost parameters that are susceptible to being influenced by public policy and institutional arrangements. From a cost perspective, two distinct strategies can be used for raising private or fiscal rates of return. One is to shift costs from one actor to another. For example, when public authorities pay for courses, private returns rise. This is not always a zero-sum game: a reduction in direct costs for a low income individual that raises private returns and thereby the incentive to study might result in increased participation and hence a rise in both private and fiscal gains. A key implication from the analysis is that someone – employers and/or governments – may have to share costs to at least some extent in order for private returns to be high enough to create this kind of incentive. (Issues surrounding cost sharing are discussed in Section 4 below.)

Conversely, under certain conditions the private returns to individuals are likely to be so high that they can afford to pay a larger share of the cost.

A second strategy is to reduce the costs of study absolutely, for example through a more efficient learning process, through more individualised and self-paced instruction or through greater focus on achieving desired learning outcomes. However, the potential gain from such improvements is hard to estimate, not least because implementing them requires developmental costs.[14] The above analysis has demonstrated the effect of a more clear-cut means of reducing costs: using accreditation of prior learning so that adult students can reduce study time (see Bjørnåvold, 2002; Duvekot, 2002).[15] One current example of this is the Norwegian policy that gives adults with work experience who never completed upper secondary education direct access to university studies (OECD, 2002b).

The analysis also serves to highlight two important gaps in empirical evidence:

- The paucity of evidence on what happens to earnings after individuals participate in learning activities. The data in Box 4.2 suggesting that Canadians who acquire degrees in midlife see a steep rise in their earnings raise further questions. Are there similar patterns in other countries? Are the outcomes of learning similar for other age groups? What is the relative importance of changing jobs, and changing employers, in driving the large rise in earnings? And what about the case of persons who participate in learning activities *not* leading to formal education qualifications? If rises for them are less dramatic, is this because the activity is of less value, or simply less visible?

- The lack of information on current practices in accrediting prior learning, including the number of adult learners who benefit from APL, the extent to which they are granted academic credit, the costs of APL, the credibility of APL practices among education providers and employers, or the ultimate impact on the duration and quality of studies. Without such information it is difficult to evaluate the real potential of APL as a tool to facilitate the substitution of non-formal for formal learning.

4. IMPROVING FINANCIAL SUSTAINABILITY

Even if policy makers succeed in strengthening incentives to invest in lifelong learning, there is still the issue of whether the two critical actors – employers and individuals – will have the *financial means* to act on those incentives. This section reviews the nature of this problem and examines approaches that have been undertaken in several countries around the notion of sharing the costs of learning, or "co-financing".

For initial education by young people, funding constraints on individuals have been reduced by government interventions such as grants, direct funding of institutions to minimise fees, and student loans. For adult learning, there are less well established conventions and institutional arrangements for public support. Factors that might make the cost of capital prohibitively expensive for individuals include high interest rates on unsecured loans for cost of living expenses, reliance on after-tax savings, or foregone returns on alternative investments. The rest of this section considers the mechanisms used in the past, and reviews some of the initiatives currently being tried.

4.1 Overview of past approaches

Problems in financing lifelong learning have for several decades revolved around the difficulty of enabling adults to take a break from gainful employment while learning. "Recurrent education", conceived as a "right" for individuals in the 1960s and 1970s (see OECD/CERI, 1976 and Papadopoulos, 1995) never became an enduring widespread practice partly for lack of adequate funding. Another underlying difficulty was the failure of "training markets" to emerge as anticipated, because the

---

14. Information on policy initiatives to reduce the costs of lifelong learning and increase its benefits is included in OECD (2000; 2001c).

15. The potential importance of reduced study time is also evident in other analysis: "if the average length of tertiary studies were shortened by one year without compromising quality, the internal rate of return for males in the countries under review would increase by 1 to 5 percentage points ... to achieve the same increase via wage differentiation would require an increase in the tertiary wage premium by 5 to 14 percentage points" (OECD, 2002a, p. 127).

educational landscape was dominated by formal education systems that functioned as traditional public providers.

Public authorities had during the 1970s and early 1980s attempted to increase learning *supply* through "revenue-generating" levies that raised money through payroll taxes imposed by governments or through collective agreements, used to enhance training organisations, typically governed by social partners. Meanwhile *demand* for learning activity was stimulated by two general approaches: a "levy exemption scheme" for employers (Gasskov, 1998), and vouchers for individuals (West *et al.*, 2000). The "levy exemption scheme", pioneered in the French law of 1971, encouraged firms to provide training directly by deducting training expenditures from the training element of the payroll tax.[16]

More clearly defined education and training markets have emerged in recent years, helped by the belief in a need for greater heterogeneity of provision, and by the perception that the changes sweeping economies and enterprises created a new need for a more qualified workforce and that therefore investment would generate substantial returns. This renewed "training market paradigm" has provided a framework for the search for means to ensure a sustainable level of investment in lifelong learning (OECD, 2001*c*).

4.2 Strategies for co-financing lifelong learning

Since the late 1990s, there has been growing consensus in policy discussions that:

- public authorities alone could not provide the necessary financial resources for lifelong learning;

- as the adult learning component generates considerable private returns, employers and employees should finance at least some of it;

- as employers already finance work-related learning by employees to a large extent, more attention needs to be given to learning that is not related to the current employment of individuals, and to learning for which returns are shared; and

- greater reliance on market forces could strengthen the incentives both for learners to seek more efficient learning options, and for providers to achieve higher levels of efficiency.

This has contributed to the view that strategies for financing lifelong learning need to involve a partnership between private individuals and others, replacing simple calls for more public funding of courses. This has not been based solely on the limits to what public money will or should pay for, but perhaps more importantly on a rethinking of individual learning behaviour. Given low levels of participation among the least qualified, even where opportunities are available at little or no cost, doubts have arisen over whether it is just lack of resources that discourages individual participation. One hypothesis is that having no financial stake in learning diminishes individuals' sense of "ownership" of, and hence responsibility for, their development. A related argument is that economic self-sufficiency requires a sense of building up *assets*, including human capital, which gives poorer groups more of a vested interest in society (Sherraden, 2001; Boshara, 2001).

A consequent search for new models of financing investment has revolved around the issue of *co-financing* by individuals, governments, and employers. The OECD, in co-operation with the European Learning Account Project,[17] has been working to fill a gap in knowledge about what forms of co-financing exist today. These initiatives cover a wide spectrum of activity.[18] Some have emerged as attempts to address problems that were not adequately addressed by earlier approaches to financing adult education and training. More generally, they reflect a willingness of public authorities, social partners and non-governmental organisations to try new approaches that are consistent with the learner-centred and demand-driven orientation of lifelong learning. They aim to strengthen incentives and financial means for individuals to engage in learning – particularly those for whom costs have been a barrier to participation. The initiatives can be grouped according to three general objectives (see Table 4.3).

---

16. For more information on the various approaches tried, see Gasskov (1994).

17. The European Learning Account Project was set up in 1999 with the support of the United Kingdom Department for Education and Skills and subsequently by the National Learning and Skills Council of England. For further details see Cheesman (2002).

18. Unless otherwise indicated, the information in this section is taken from OECD (2003*c*).

CHAPTER 4

STRATEGIES FOR SUSTAINABLE INVESTMENT
IN ADULT LIFELONG LEARNING

Table 4.3 Co-financing mechanisms: objectives, types of measures, and country initiatives

Measures	Objectives		
	Reducing direct costs to individuals	Reducing foregone earnings	Sharing risk
Savings accounts and individual learning accounts	Netherlands, 2001; United Kingdom, 2000; (discontinued in 2001, relaunched in Wales, planned to be relaunched in Scotland); Basque region of Spain, 2000; Belgium (Flanders), 2003	Skandia, 1999 Swedish government (proposed in 2000; not yet finalised)	
Time accounts		Germany; France (collective agreements)	
Interest rate subsidy	Korea, 2002		
Tax deductions and tax credits	Austria, 2002 Netherlands, 2001 Sweden (in development)	Skandia; Netherlands, 1993	
Income-contingent loans			Australia (undergraduate higher education, 1989; post-graduate, 2002)
Transferable training loans			United Kingdom (in development)

Source: OECD (2003c).

Objective 1: *Reducing direct costs to individuals*

The objective of most co-financing schemes is to leverage the resources that individuals put into learning (in cash or time) with a matching contribution and/or eligibility for reduced fees. Examples include:

• The English Individual Learning Account (ILA) Programme, launched in September 2000. Under this initiative, when individuals contributed £25 to set up an account, that was matched by £150 of public money that could be used to buy courses from approved training providers. Following an initial slow start, the Government supplemented the scheme by compensating training providers to offer 80% discounts to accountholders taking courses in ICT and mathematics, and 20% discounts on other courses. The target of reaching one million ILAs was reached well ahead of schedule, in May 2001. In October 2001, notice was given of the withdrawl of the programme in England due to demand exceeding expectations and increasing complaints about the ways in which ILAs were being marketed and the value-for-money being offered by some learning providers; the programme then closed in November following allegations of fraudulent use of ILAs by some learning providers.

• The Ministry of Education in the Netherlands established a series of pilot projects in March 2001 that were intended to run for a year. The initiatives provided a lump sum of 450 euro to each individual opening an account to cover direct training costs. Individuals and their employers could supplement the initial sum. The initiatives were managed by a variety of institutions: industrial sector training funds; regional education bureaus; and regional education centres. A second round was initiated in 2002 and scheduled to run to the end of 2003. It differed from the earlier initiative insofar as it required that 35% of accountholders be unemployed; it also excluded collective courses.

- The Basque region in Spain established a Learning Account Programme in September 2000 to test the feasibility of using training credits to enhance individual choice in lifelong learning. Individuals contribute 25% of the cost and public authorities 75%. It was originally targeted at vocational teachers in the Vocational Training Centres to strengthen their ICT skills. A smaller initiative established learning accounts for the unemployed. At the end of 2001 the learning account initiative for vocational teachers was extended to secondary school teachers.

- In January 2003 labour market authorities in Flanders (Belgium) launched individual learning and development accounts on a pilot basis. The accounts start with an initial contribution by the Government of 1 000 euro that can be supplemented by employers and/or individuals, and can be used to cover direct costs of education and training (tuition, books), related costs (counselling and recognition/certification of acquired competencies) as well as indirect costs (transportation and childcare).

Another approach is to reduce the cost of capital for investment in learning through interest rate subsidies or taxation concessions:

- The Ministry of Education and Human Resources Development in Korea established an initiative in 2002 that offers interest rate subsidies to adults (age 27-64) taking out loans to cover the cost of tuition for long-term training (more than one year) in private technical institutions. Learners are entitled to take out loans from private banks to cover the full cost. Interest costs are split between the government and individuals. This parallels loans that are available through the Vocational Ability Development Programme operated by the Ministry of Labour as part of the Employment Insurance Programme that was implemented in 1995. Learners pay 1% interest and the duration of payment is equal to the duration of studies.

- The Austrian government adopted an initiative in 2002 that liberalised earlier provisions for both employers and employees by allowing them to deduct learning-related expenses from taxable income. This reduces the cost of capital by enabling costs to be paid out of *before-tax earnings*. Employers are now allowed to deduct 120% of training costs from profits as an operating cost (previously they were allowed to deduct 100%). Those who do not earn a profit are entitled to a tax credit of 6% that can be applied to tax liabilities for earlier or subsequent years. Individuals are allowed to deduct from taxable income the costs of education and training that qualifies them for new forms of employment as well as that required for their present job (previously only the former costs were deductible).

- In the Netherlands there is an employee savings scheme under which individuals are allowed to set aside an amount each year of before-tax earnings up to a designated limit (613 euro in 2003) to cover certain investment-related expenditure, including that for educational purposes. An additional scheme is under consideration that would allow individuals to defer a portion of their income, to be taken during a leave of absence.

Objective 2: Reducing foregone earnings

There are two general approaches to replacing income for individuals who stop work to pursue full-time learning activities. One is to set aside a share of working hours (*e.g.* overtime) in a "time account" that can be drawn on to continue earnings while an individual learns. The other is to set aside a share of earnings in a financial account, again to be used to replace earnings during periods of education or training.

"Time accounts" are seen frequently now in collective agreements in Germany. One of the earliest was established in 1988 in Deutsche Shell AG in the framework of an agreement under which the regular work week was reduced from 40 hours to 38 or 37.5 hours. Under that scheme individuals were entitled to apply the reduced hours to a time account that would continue to pay their wages while workers participated in training that was not necessarily linked to their present job. Since then the principle of co-financing has been incorporated into a number of schemes. In 2001, Auto 5000 GmbH, a subsidiary of Volkswagen AG, negotiated an agreement for a new assembly plant that hired previously unemployed workers. Under the agreement, which includes a strong emphasis on training, individuals spend an average of 3 hours per week in training, half paid by the employer, and half out of their personal time. Under a hybrid scheme established by the Frankfurt am Main airport authority, individuals are entitled to a 600 euro training voucher that may be used to pay for training chosen by them, on the condition that it occurs in their personal time.

Though they have been debated extensively, financial accounts to replace earnings during periods of learning are rare. Insofar as the total sums are necessarily larger (foregone earnings tend to be much greater than direct costs of education and training), such schemes need to take a long-term time horizon for savings. One case of actual experience is that of Skandia, a Sweden-based insurance multinational that in 1999 set up a scheme under which employees who set aside up to 20% of their annual salary in a *competence assurance* scheme, had their contributions matched by the company. The funds in the scheme were to be used to replace earnings when employees stopped work to participate in mutually-agreed learning activities. The scheme was modified over time (to facilitate inter-firm mobility), and was eventually adopted by other Swedish companies as part of Skandia's line of financial products.

The Swedish government has been working on a scheme that is more modest in scale. Under the proposed scheme individuals would be allowed to deduct from taxable income up to a quarter of the amount contributed to an individual learning account, with a ceiling of SEK 9 500 (approximately 1 000 euro). Money withdrawn would be taxed as ordinary income; however when withdrawals are related to costs of learning and skill development, a certain amount would be tax deductible, and individuals would receive up to SEK 1 000 (about 110 euro) as a tax credit. Another scheme in Sweden, the Adult Education Initiative, was introduced in 1997. While not based on co-financing, it does build on the principle of offering income support during education training by providing grants (equal to the level of unemployment benefits) to poorly qualified adults 25-55 years to allow them to complete upper secondary education (the education programmes are available at no charge). It was part of a major national initiative to raise adult qualifications levels quickly.

Objective 3: Sharing risk

A final grouping of co-financing strategies includes those that aim to reduce the risk to individuals of investing in learning, by sharing it with others. For example, Australia introduced income-contingent loans for higher education fees in 1989: the higher education contribution scheme (HECS) for undergraduate studies. Under current HECS arrangements students pay about 30% of the average cost of a place, and the cost varies by field of study. Students can either choose to pay the HECS directly to the university when they enrol and receive a 25% discount, or defer payment. Students who defer payment begin repaying their debt through the income tax system when their income reaches the minimum threshold (which was A$24 365 or about 14 000 euro in 2002-03). The repayments commence at 3% of taxable income, and the higher the income, the faster the rate of repayment (to a maximum of 6%). Thus, the government assumes the risk for those individuals whose earnings after study are exceptionally low (*i.e.* who do not reach the threshold level for repayment). In 2002 the government extended the principle of income-contingent loans to a wider group of learners by establishing the Postgraduate Education Loans Scheme (PELS).

In addition to the risk to individuals of low returns from learning activities, there is a related risk to employers of low returns due to "poaching" (individuals leaving before an employer receives the benefits of the investment in training). As part of its "workforce development strategies" the United Kingdom Learning and Skills Council is considering launching a pilot project featuring transferable training loans to address the problem of diminished employer returns due to poaching (as well as cash-flow for small companies). A transferable training loan is intended to overcome these problems by creating a debt when an individual undergoes education or training, and which is tied to that individual for the period that it is amortized. If the individual stays with a company, the company would be paying off the loan as a kind of depreciation. If the individual leaves, the new employer under the scheme being considered would pick up the debt. The rationale for doing so would be that paying the debt is cheaper than poaching a diminishing volume of skills in the open market. It is anticipated that if the scheme is implemented, it would be tried out in a sector dominated by small companies in which there is a limited number of licensed occupations and where employers can agree to a membership or regulatory tracking mechanism.

4.3 Results and lessons to date

Strategies for co-financing lifelong learning are relatively recent, limited in number and still largely untested in terms of their long-term costs and benefits. Initiatives such as Learn $ave in Canada that incorporate an experimental design to assess the impact of co-financing mechanisms are rare. However, various pilots such as those in the Basque region of Spain, the Netherlands and the United Kingdom, have been established for the express purpose of evaluating whether the initiatives should be continued and expanded. Nevertheless, although there are few published evaluations to date, it is possible to draw some tentative lessons.

Individual incentives and motivation

Generally, the schemes have been successful as tools for enhancing individual choice in pursuing learning opportunities. The Basque learning account pilot for vocational teachers, for example, was used by almost 40% of staff. The English Individual Learning Account Programme, after a slow start, reached its objective of 1 million accounts in less than half the time expected, and peaked at 2.6 million account holders before shutting down because of the irregularities noted above.[19] An earlier initiative in England, the Learning Account Scheme, was established in Gloucestershire in the mid-1990s as one of a number of pilots run by the Training and Enterprise Councils. It matched contributions by individuals to a training account that was managed by a local bank, when individuals spent money on recognised training expenses. The scheme reached persons who, as a group, participated comparatively less in training, and was particularly effective in reaching women who were returning to the labour force. The Adult Education Initiative in Sweden proved to be very effective in reaching 800 000 adults (nearly a quarter of the population in that age group). In the Netherlands, the eight co-financing pilot projects, which were intended to serve poorly qualified individuals, were largely successful in establishing the intended number of accounts, and encouraging accountholders to pursue studies.

A second-round pilot in the Netherlands initiative and another in the Basque region aimed at the unemployed encountered more difficulties in reaching their targets; partly because individuals preferred moving into employment at the first opportunity (the co-financing schemes did not cover cost of living), and also because the newness of the schemes meant that knowledge about them was limited.

There is a pivotal question of whether co-financing schemes can influence the likelihood of those who are least qualified – and most under-represented in further education and training – to contribute and participate more in their own learning activities. The experience of untargeted schemes, such as the Individual Learning Account Programme in England, is not particularly encouraging; those with no qualifications comprised only a small share (16%) of all account holders. Schemes aimed at the unemployed, such as in the Netherlands, seem to have difficulty in reaching their targets, though possibly for reasons that are unrelated to the effect of financial incentives.

In drawing overall conclusions it is important to differentiate between initiatives in terms of whether they target particular groups or not, and whether they provide income support. The Adult Education Initiative in Sweden proved to be effective in reaching large numbers of poorly qualified adults. The experience of Skandia in trying to attract poorly qualified adults into learning activities is also instructive. When the scheme was implemented, it included a 3:1 contribution of company funding for poorly educated workers (9 years of education or less), 45 years old or older, and who had been with Skandia for at least 15 years. After three years, 43% of persons with less than an upper secondary education had set up accounts, compared to 20% of those with an

---

19. The English Skills Strategy, introduced in July 2003, builds on lessons from the Individual Learning Account Programme. The strategy broadens free training opportunities for low skilled adults, and increases choice in learning in order to lift participation, while ensuring some quality controls are maintained (Secretary of State for Education and Skills, 2003).

upper secondary education and 48% of those with a tertiary education (Hansson and Färm, 2002).

Framework conditions, administration and support

A key difference between co-financing mechanisms and other forms of finance is in the interactive role played by individuals. Indeed, the logic behind co-financing mechanisms is that if individuals play an active role in financing investments in themselves, they will play an active role in deciding where and how to invest. The implication is that the net financial value of support is not the only consideration; it is important to also consider the degree to which individuals are "empowered" to play an active role in investing in their own development, and that depends on the details of the institutional arrangements.

A common feature of co-financing mechanisms is the presence of a third party to bring together the individual and the education or training provider. Sometimes that third party has been quite literally distinct, as in the case of a bank or other financial institution (examples include projects in the Netherlands and England). Frequently it has been in the form of an existing education and training authority assuming a separate role of managing a form of learning account (*e.g.* another pilot in the Netherlands, and a project in the Basque region in Spain). Sometimes the schemes involve direct payments from accounts to education and training institutions chosen by the individual learner. Another approach (as in the Individual Learning Accounts in the United Kingdom) has been for the government to effectively match individual payments while also giving individuals access to specific courses at a discount.

Accountability is an issue that arises as one moves away from single-party financing to co-financing. It is an issue that has been more complicated by pressure to put large innovations into place quickly. Where direct contributions have been involved, the most common approach to preserve accountability has been for the co-financing partner to match individual contributions at the time of the transaction to purchase education or training services. This has minimised the risk that funds are spent on activities that are not allowable. In the case of the private sector scheme in Skandia, there was concern that investment decisions should be mutually agreed to by employers and employees when both pay; but there was recognition as well that such agreement might not always be possible. The remedy has been to establish separate employer and employee funds.

In addressing the issue of accountability, however, there has also been concern about ensuring that co-financing systems were sufficiently "user-friendly", especially insofar as such schemes were aiming to reach persons who do not typically participate in learning activities. This concern has been met through the use of telephone "help-lines" (*e.g.* in the United Kingdom), and support to individuals in drawing up development plans (*e.g.* Skandia).

It remains to be seen whether the various new mechanisms for co-financing lifelong learning are sufficiently user-friendly, well-funded, and mutually beneficial to make a difference in the willingness of individuals to invest in learning, and in the quality of the outcomes of such activities. The evaluations that are now underway should provide useful insights. At this point though, there appears to be a significant level of interest in using finance mechanisms that spread responsibility between individuals and others.

5. CONCLUSIONS AND POLICY PRIORITIES

Lifelong learning is a core strategy for facilitating the transition to a knowledge society, and ensuring that the social and economic benefits of a knowledge society are equitably distributed. However, the timing, duration, and cost of the adult learning component of the lifelong learning framework, as well as the distribution of its benefits, are different from those that apply to systems of initial education and training. These differences threaten the economic and financial sustainability of the continuing growth of lifelong learning, as well as its social acceptance over the long term. This chapter has discussed an analytical framework for evaluating strategies for ensuring the economic sustainability of lifelong learning, and considered ways to improve its financial sustainability.

Simulations of rates of return to investment in lifelong learning for adults provide a framework within which it is possible to evaluate different policy scenarios. They make it possible to see that improved visibility and recognition of prior learning has a positive impact on economic sustainability. By reducing the duration of learning activities this reduces the economic cost of foregone earnings and production, and the non-economic cost of foregone leisure. They also suggest that other policies that facilitate co-financing can influence private and fiscal rates of return by shifting costs. Finally, they indicate what policy conditions need to be met in order to justify sharing of costs.

There appears to be substantial risk of underinvestment in lifelong learning because individuals, employers, or governments shoulder a financial burden that is disproportionate to the distribution of benefits. This asymmetry between benefits and costs is due to risk and uncertainty, capital market failures, and a mismatch between the supply-oriented nature of past financing strategies and the demand-driven nature of lifelong learning. It is compounded by the scale of financial implications of lifelong learning in the case of adults who cease employment while learning. Recent innovations are attempting to deal with these problems through strategies that reduce direct costs to individuals, reduce the burden of foregone earnings, or reduce the cost of risk.

Further progress towards enhancing economic and financial sustainability of lifelong learning depends on action across diverse areas:

- For adults, reductions in the duration of formal learning activities are critical. Further attention needs to be given to the robustness, accessibility, transparency, predictability, and cost of techniques for assessing and recognising skills, competencies, and knowledge acquired outside formal education and training systems. Progress in this area would reduce the duration of more formal learning activities and also foster emergence of less structured and potentially less costly alternatives.

- The chapter provides further evidence that the low level of participation in lifelong learning by poorly qualified adults may be explained in part by comparatively weaker economic incentives, and their more limited access to financing arrangements that are consistent with their needs and preferences. Both groups of factors are susceptible to policy influence.

- The financial implications of making lifelong learning a reality for all are large and seem to exceed the capacity of present financial mechanisms. Some rationalisation is needed to ensure that public resources are available for activities that generate substantial social returns (as in the case of poorly qualified adults acquiring basic skills), and to ensure that the incentives to invest in lifelong learning are aligned appropriately with incentives for other forms of investment. Aside from providing financial support the public sector needs to consider how to create and enhance the framework conditions to make it easier for social partners to share financial burdens.

- There is a need to monitor the considerable experimentation presently going on with respect to mechanisms for co-financing lifelong learning to better understand what works best for different types of individuals and enterprises.

References

BASSI, L., LUDWIG, J., MCMURRER, D. and **VAN BUREN, M.** (2000), *Profiting from Learning: Do Firms' Investments in Education and Training Pay Off?*, American Society for Training and Development, Alexandria, VA.

BATEMAN, A. and **KNIGHT, B.** (2003), *Giving Credit: A Review of RPL and Credit Transfer in the Vocational Education and Training Sector, 1995 to 2001*, National Centre for Vocational Education Research, Adelaide, South Australia.

BJØRNÅVOLD, J. (2002), "Assessment of non-formal learning: a link to strategies for lifelong learning", in D. Colardyn (ed.), *Lifelong Learning: Which Ways Forward*, Kenniscentrum EVC and Lemma Publishers, Utrecht.

BLÖNDAL, S., FIELD, S. and **GIROUARD, N.** (2002), "Investment in human capital through upper-secondary and tertiary education", OECD *Economic Studies*, No. 34 2002/1, pp. 41-89, Paris.

BOSHARA, R. (ed.) (2001), *Building Assets: A Report on the Asset-Development and IDA Field*, Corporation for Enterprise Development, Washington, D.C.

CHEESMAN, K. (2002), *European Learning Account Project: A Report on the Activities of the ELAP Project*, European Learning Account Partners Network, London (mimeo).

COHN, E. and **ADDISON, J.** (1998), "The economic returns to lifelong learning in OECD countries", *Education Economics*, Vol. 6, No. 3, pp. 253-307.

COLARDYN, D. (ed.) (2002), *Lifelong Learning: Which Ways Forward*, Kenniscentrum EVC and Lemma Publishers, Utrecht.

DUVEKOT, R. (2002), "The dynamics of non-formal learning and the opening-up of national learning systems", in D. Colardyn (ed.), *Lifelong Learning: Which Ways Forward*, Kenniscentrum EVC and Lemma Publishers, Utrecht.

GASSKOV, V. (ed.) (1994), *Alternative Schemes for Financing Training*, International Labour Office, Geneva.

GASSKOV, V. (1998), "Levies, leave and collective agreements incentives for enterprises and individuals to invest in training", *Vocational Training: European Journal*, No. 13, January-April, pp. 27-36.

HANSSON, L. and **FÄRM, K.** (2002), *Kompetenskonton – den första utvärderingen*, prepared for Svenskt Näringsliv (Confederation of Swedish Enterprise), Stockholm.

JENKINS, A., VIGNOLES, A., WOLF, A. and **GALINDO-RUEDA, F.** (2002), *The Determinants and Effects of Lifelong Learning*, Centre for the Economics of Education, London School of Economics and Political Science, London.

MELLANDER, E. and **SKEDINGER, P.** (1999), "Corporate job ladders in Europe: wage premia for university vs. high school level positions", *Swedish Economic Policy Review*, Vol. 6, pp. 449-487.

OECD (1993), *Industry Training in Australia, Sweden and the United States*, Paris.

OECD (1998a), *Education at a Glance: OECD Indicators 1998*, Paris.

OECD (1998b), *Human Capital Investment: An International Comparison*, Paris.

OECD (2000), *Where are the resources for lifelong learning?*, Paris.

OECD (2001a), *Starting Strong: Early Childhood Education and Care*, Paris.

OECD (2001b), "Lifelong learning for all: policy directions", *Education Policy Analysis* 2001, pp. 9-42, Paris.

OECD (2001c), *Economics and Finance of Lifelong Learning*, Paris.

OECD (2002a), *Education at a Glance: OECD Indicators 2002*, Paris.

OECD (2002b), *Reviews of National Policies for Education: Lifelong Learning in Norway*, Paris.

OECD (2003a), *Beyond Rhetoric: Adult Learning Policies and Practices*, Paris.

OECD (2003b), "Upgrading workers' skills and competencies", in *Employment Outlook* 2003, Paris.

OECD (2003c), *Taking Stock of Co-finance Mechanisms* (updated), www.oecd.org

OECD/CERI (Centre for Educational Research and Innovation) (1976), *Developments in Educational Leave of Absence*, OECD/CERI, Paris.

OECD and **U.S. DEPARTMENT OF EDUCATION** (1997), *Adult Learning*, U.S. Government Printing Office, Washington, DC.

OTTERSTEIN, E., LINDH, T. and **MELLANDER, E.** (1999), "Evaluating firm training, effects on performance, and labour demand", *Applied Economic Letters*, Vol. 6, pp. 431-437.

PAPADOPOULOS, G. (1995), *Education 1960-1990: The OECD Perspective*, OECD, Paris.

SECRETARY OF STATE FOR EDUCATION AND SKILLS (2003), *21st Century Skills: Realising Our Potential – Individuals, Employers, Nation*, Department of Education and Skills, London.

SHERRADEN, M. (2001), "Asset-building policy and programs for the poor", in T. Shapiro and E. Wolff (eds.), *Assets for the Poor: The Benefits of Spreading Asset Ownership*, Russell Sage Foundation, New York.

TUIJNMAN, A. (1989), *Recurrent Education, Earnings, and Well-being: A Fifty-year Longitudinal Study of a Cohort of Swedish Men*, Alqvist and Wiksell, Stockholm.

WEST, A., SPARKES, J., BALABANOV, T. and **ROGERS, S.** (2000), *Demand-side Financing – A Focus on Vouchers in Post-Compulsory Education and Training: Discussion Paper and Case Studies*, European Centre for the Development of Vocational Education (CEDEFOP), Thessaloniki.

WHEELAHAN, L., DENNIS, N., FIRTH, J., MILLER, P., NEWTON, D., PASCOE, S. and **VEENKER, P.** (2002), *Recognition of Prior Learning: Policy and Practice in Australia*, Australian Qualifications Framework, Melbourne.

WURZBURG, G. and **DE SOUSA, M.** (2002), "Financing mechanisms for VET", in Korea Research Institute for Vocational Education and Training (ed.), *The KRIVET International Conference on Vocational Education and Training*, pp. 85-137, Seoul.

Data for the Figure
CHAPTER 4

Data for Figure 4.1

Average annual earnings by educational attainment and whether obtained highest qualification in the 1993-98 period, 30-49 year-olds, Canada (Canadian $)

	Year 1	Year 2	Year 3	Year 4	Year 5
University degree, no study in period	29 493	33 132	34 128	35 379	37 189
University degree, obtained in Year 3	27 858	24 780	28 604	33 797	37 667
College certificate, no study in period	20 594	22 512	23 129	24 346	24 967
College certificate, obtained in Year 3	18 675	19 024	18 582	24 171	25 489
High school diploma, no study in period	17 584	19 574	20 011	21 032	21 652

Source: OECD Secretariat analysis of data from the Canadian Survey of Labour and Income Dynamics, 1993-98 panel.

ANNEX: Recent education policy developments in OECD countries

This Annex contains summaries of recent education policy developments in OECD member countries. The summaries, which were supplied by countries on a voluntary basis, are intended to provide an overview of major developments and sources where further information can be found.

Countries were invited to submit the summaries based on standard guidelines. The maximum length was 200 words per country. Due to space constraints, the entries have not been able to cover all significant policy developments. The emphasis was on outlining major education policy developments that have occurred recently or which are being implemented, and which are likely to be of most interest to an international audience. Countries were asked to be selective, and were not required to cover each education sector or level. The first part of each entry outlines the basic administratrive structure of education. Contact details are provided where interested readers can obtain more information about the reforms concerned. The entries have been edited to provide a consistent format and observe space constraints.

Summaries were provided by 18 countries: Austria; Belgium (French-speaking Community); Canada; Denmark; Finland; France; Germany; Ireland; Italy; Japan; Korea; the Netherlands; New Zealand; Norway; Portugal; Spain; the United Kingdom; and the United States.

The summaries emphasise the broad scope of education policy making in OECD countries. The countries have highlighted policy developments within a framework of lifelong learning, ranging from early childhood and preschool education (*e.g.* Austria, Korea and New Zealand) through to adult learning and workplace training (*e.g.* Denmark, Finland and Spain). The breadth of policy initiatives makes them difficult to readily categorise, although several common themes are evident.

First, almost all the countries have drawn attention to policies intended to lift the quality of learning in the compulsory school years. This emphasis has included more clearly specifying the key skills and knowledge that students need to achieve [*e.g.* Belgium (French community), Germany and Japan], introducing external evaluations of student learning and school performance (*e.g.* the Netherlands, Norway and Portugal), and strengthening teacher expertise (*e.g.* in teaching reading in the United States). The adoption of frameworks that specify learning objectives and accountability requirements have generally been part of a broader reform package that also provides schools with more operational autonomy (*e.g.* in Finland and Italy).

Second, issues of social disadvantage and student alienation continue to be major concerns, with programmes aimed at reducing the number of young people without qualifications (*e.g.* France and Germany), improving student motivation (*e.g.* the United Kingdom), or reducing differences in education opportunities across regions (*e.g.* Korea).

Third, the higher education sector has been a particular focus of reform in most countries. These changes have generally been in the direction of providing institutions with more autonomy within a framework of greater external accountability for performance (see Chapter 3 of this volume for more details). Within Europe a major impetus for higher education reform has been the Bologna Declaration with its goal of a common framework of higher education degrees, and several countries have drawn attention to changes in the structure of their higher education qualifications (Denmark, Germany, the Netherlands and Norway). Finally, the organisation and administration of the education sector is undergoing substantial change in a number of countries. The moves towards greater operational autonomy for education institutions and more involvement by local authorities mean that central education departments are becoming less involved in the direct provision of education, and more focused on strategic planning and the evaluation of outcomes.

AUSTRIA

Austria's school system is centrally organised within a federal political structure. It has a high degree of internal differentiation, different school types, and a range of transfer arrangements between schools. Currently, efforts are being made to adjust the educational system to the requirements of the knowledge-based society and to establish a system of lifelong learning. Reforms of pre-elementary institutions, of the transition from school to work, of adult learning, life and career guidance, teacher employment, and financing of lifelong learning are supported by OECD review visits. Quality development and assurance is one of the priorities (*www.qis.at*). Work is under way on curricular reforms, quality standards and instruments for system monitoring. The details of forthcoming measures have been laid down in a White Paper on Quality (which will also be available in English). At elementary schools the core competencies to be taught and the appropriate teaching methods are being identified. In response to the PISA report, a large-scale campaign has been launched for the promotion of reading comprehension (*www.lesefit.at*). Other follow-up activities to PISA (*e.g.* in the field of natural sciences) are being prepared. Reforms are under way in the areas of initial teacher education, in-service-training and teaching assignments. There are concrete plans to upgrade the training institutes for compulsory school teachers to university level, and compulsory in-service training for teachers is at the trial stage. The new University Act of October 2002 provides universities with more autonomy and leeway for action (*www.unigesetz.at*). New areas of university autonomy include recruitment of personnel, financial planning (encompassing guaranteed public funding) and organisational structures.

BELGIUM (French-speaking Community)

A federated entity of Belgium, the French Community is responsible for education policy for the entire French-speaking region of the country (the Walloon Region and the bilingual Brussels Capital Region). During the school year 2001-2002, around 490 000 pupils were in elementary education (nursery and primary), 350 000 in secondary education and 140 000 in higher education (university or other). The main reform in the area of compulsory education (6 to 18 years of age) was in July 1997 with the introduction of legislation on the priority objectives for education. It defined clearly for the first time what those objectives were and, in a related measure, the Parliament for the French Community identified core skills to be achieved by all pupils at key stages of their education. A new education steering structure was set up to accompany the reform. As well as the above, a range of legislative and regulatory measures was introduced in order to ensure equal opportunities, including a positive discrimination policy and measures to assist new students, including immigrants. In higher education, basic teacher training was reformed to include 13 specific competencies with a view to attaining genuine professional status. A reform of continuing training was also adopted instituting rights and duties for teachers. Further information is available from: *www.cfwb.be* and *www.agers.cwfb.be* and *www.restode.cwfb.be*

CANADA

Politically, Canada is a confederation of ten provinces and three territories, each of which, within the federal system of shared powers, is constitutionally responsible for education. Canada does not have a central ministry, department, or office of education. It is difficult to provide a succinct overview of major education policy developments throughout Canada. The Council of Ministers of Education, Canada (CMEC) gateway (*www.educationcanada.cmec.ca*) provides information about education. The website includes links to key governments and organisations that form the core of the Canadian learning community.

DENMARK

Responsibility for education is shared between the Ministry of Education, municipal councils and school boards. In 2001 the government established the Ministry of Science, Technology and Innovation to enhance interaction between business and the worlds of research and education. The responsibility for universities was transferred to the new ministry. The Ministry of Education still has the responsibility for non-university higher education (see *www.uvm.dk* and *www.vtu.dk*). A new university bill introduced a reform of governance designed to enhance universities' exchange of knowledge with economy and society. The main changes in university governance involve: a Governing Board with external majority; appointed leaders (Rector and Deans) rather than elected leaders; increased self-government;

strengthening of internal quality controls; and implementation of the objectives of the Bologna declaration on higher education. Several years ago non-university tertiary education institutions were offered the option of being merged into "Centres for Tertiary Education" (CVU). These centres provide education, in-service training and consultancy services in specified fields. The 2003 "Act on Career Guidance and Counselling" set targets and standards for counselling and guidance, restructured the training of counsellors to give them cross-sectoral skills, established the "National Centre for Education and Career Guidance" and cross-municipal centres for guidance related to post-compulsory education. Improved guidance and counselling is an important element in strengthening vocational education and training in particular. The government has set up a cross-ministerial committee to investigate policies to improve social mobility and diminish the negative effects of disadvantaged social backgrounds.

FINLAND

Education is the responsibility of the Ministry of Education in collaboration with municipalities. During the 1990s national control of compulsory and upper secondary level education was eased, and education providers now have considerable operational autonomy within national guidelines and objectives. This new operational culture entails rigorous evaluation of education. Formerly, the National Board of Education was in charge of the national evaluation of education, as well as the development of education enforcing the national core curricula. A separate Education Evaluation Council was established within the Ministry of Education in 2003 (see www.minedu.fi). The Finnish polytechnics are professionally-oriented higher education institutions that operate alongside universities. In 2003 Parliament passed the new Polytechnics Act which is intended to clarify their tasks and provide more operational autonomy. Polytechnics and universities together form the higher education system, and both have their own profiles. The tasks of the polytechnics consist of teaching, applied research and development; they also have a role in regional development (see www.minedu.fi). The size of the working-age population is declining as the post-war baby-boom generation reaches retirement. To alleviate the envisaged labour shortage and increase the employment rate, the Government launched a five-year programme in 2003 to promote the employability and career development of adults with no more than compulsory education. The programme will increase the supply of vocational and information technology education. Additional measures have been created to support adult studies, and to lift participation and completion rates (see www.minedu.fi).

FRANCE

The Ministry of Education is responsible for education, and almost all education funding is provided by the State. In education the focus of French government policy is on two broad themes: endeavouring to ensure that all students succeed; and placing the emphasis on quality in adapting the education system. Achieving these objectives has involved the development of policies and programmes focusing on the following priorities in particular: preventing and combating illiteracy; improving education in citizenship and combating all forms of violence in schools; providing better conditions for the education of handicapped and sick pupils and students; sharply reducing the number of drop-outs with no qualifications; reasserting the value of the teaching profession; improving linkages between general and vocational education; counteracting failure in the first cycle of university education; promoting student mobility; promoting the image of science and careers in science; and improving initial teacher education and in-service training for teachers. At the same time, continuing efforts are being made to improve the use of new information and communication technologies in education, and to promote the early learning of foreign languages and lifelong education. For further information, see www.education.gouv.fr

GERMANY

The Federal Republic of Germany is a federal state. Responsibility for the field of general education lies with the Länder. The Federal Government is co-responsible for vocational training and higher education. In 2003, the Federal Government and the Länder initiated measures aimed at a reform of the general schools sector. These include drafting educational standards and measures to help both students with learning difficulties as well as students with particular talents. With its "Future of Education and All-Day Schools" programme, the Federal Government is helping the Länder to establish and expand all-day schools. The Federal Government and the Länder are currently discussing possibilities for a scheme of national reporting on education. The Federal Government is intensifying its efforts to halve the number of young people without training qualifications by 2010, particularly through its "Emergency Programme to Reduce Youth Unemployment" and its programme "BQF". The emergency programme encourages the integration of young people in employment. Measures to enhance the suitability of young people for vocational training include pre-vocational schemes offered by the *Länder* and government financial assistance to encourage young people to gain secondary general school-leaving (H*auptschule*) qualifications and participate in pre-vocational schemes. The BQF programme supports the disadvantaged. In the course of the Bologna process on higher education, the Bachelor/Master system has been included in the range of degree courses offered by higher education institutions. This not only involves the strengthening of the international focus of the range of courses offered in Germany, but also the reform of the content and structure of individual courses. For further information, see *www.bmbf.de* and *www.kmk.org*

IRELAND

Educational provision in Ireland is highly centralised. The Department of Education and Science, in addition to being responsible for policy development and the funding of education, also directly administers most aspects of school level education. A recent major study of the Department's operations recommended that a number of key areas of its activity should be devolved to outside agencies, thereby freeing it to focus on strategic and policy issues and on the evaluation of provision generally. Three major initiatives are currently being undertaken, arising from the recommendations of the report. First, public examinations at secondary level, previously administered by the Department are, with effect from 2003, now the responsibility of an independent State Examinations Commission; this is intended to ensure the continuing openness and capacity for development of the public examinations system. Second, the delivery of special education provision is to be reformed and enhanced through the establishment of a Special Education Council, which will have responsibility for the delivery and development of services to students with disabilities. Third, local offices are to be established in the principal regional centres in order to provide an integrated access to a range of educational services in their area. For further information see *www.education.ie*

ITALY

Italy is a parliamentary republic, a partly decentralised system. Education policy making is shared between the national government (which has responsibility for funding, school curricula, and quality control) and the Regions (responsible for education delivery, in particular for vocational education and training) (see *www.istruzione.it*). During 2002, public debate was focused on the proposed major reform of the education system. The legislation, which was passed by Parliament early 2003, affects the structure of schooling, increases the autonomy of the individual schools, and decentralises political and administrative decision making to the regional level (see *www.istruzione.it/mpi/progettoscuola*). The law extends the right to education and vocational training up to the age of 18 years. There will be two education cycles: the first cycle comprises primary school (5 years) and lower secondary school (3 years); the second cycle provides two options: the "Liceo", or general education (5 years), with direct access to university, and the system of vocational education and training (4 years) that awards a vocational qualification and allows, with a supplementary one-year course, for enrolment in university. Parallel to this legislation, a National Institute for the Evaluation of the Education System was established, and it started in 2002 with a national survey aimed at developing instruments for the regular assessment of the effectiveness of educational provision and the quality of its outputs. See *www.invalsi.it*

JAPAN

The Ministry of Education, Culture, Sports, Science and Technology (MEXT) has overall responsibility for education. MEXT offers guidance, advice and assistance to the prefectural and municipal boards of education which also carry out their respective allotted roles (see *www.mext.go.jp/english/org/struct/govern*). To support implementation of the New Course of Study, MEXT presented policies in a White Paper under the theme "Exhortation toward Learning" in 2002, and has been working on various measures to support school activities, in order to help children acquire basic knowledge and skills, think by themselves, judge and act independently, and develop their academic ability, including problem-solving ability. In response to changing expectations and demands concerning higher education, there have been substantial reforms to make universities' systems more simplified and flexible. Deliberations of the Central Council for Education have contributed to the higher education reforms. Based on the Policies for the Structural Reform of Universities (National Universities), presented by MEXT in June 2001, the following changes are now being implemented: reorganisation and merging of national universities; development of a more independent legal status and greater autonomy for national universities; and introduction of the principles of competition by using third party evaluations (see www.mext.go.jp/eky2001/index-24.html).

KOREA

The Republic of Korea has a decentralised political system. Education policy making is shared between the national government (which has responsibility for higher education, lifelong education, and national human resources development policies) and the provinces (responsible for primary and secondary education) (see "Education in Korea" at www.moe.go.kr/English). Current government priorities at school level focus on improving the basic skills for students that will enable them to function as responsible members of society. Class sizes will be reduced to 30 or less by 2008, and education for all five-year-olds will be provided free of charge by 2006. The "Comprehensive Measures to Develop Education in the Rural Areas" and the "Education Welfare Investment Priority Zone Project" will be implemented to bridge the gaps in educational quality between regions and social classes. In higher education the focus is on lifting quality so that students have world-class qualifications. New investments are planned in graduate schools and research institutes. Restructuring of university education will also take place, and poor performing institutions may be closed. A new project is being implemented to reduce the gap between higher education in Seoul and other regions, and to develop regional universities as centres of regional innovation (see "Brain Korea 21" at www.moe.go.kr/English). The Ministry of Education and Human Resources Development is focusing human resources development policies on national strategic areas such as information technology and biotechnology, finance and the law (see "HRD Strategies" at www.moe.go.kr/English).

NETHERLANDS

The Dutch education system is in general a centralised system. This centralisation is balanced by the "freedom of education": the constitutional right to found schools in accordance with one's own religious or life principles and to have these schools financed by government (see www.minocw.nl/english_oud/edusyst/). Increasing the autonomy of schools and institutions by deregulation has been a leading motive in education policy over the years. In some cases the responsibility of local municipalities has been increased (for example, in housing and programmes for the educationally disadvantaged). The main goal is to enable schools and other educational institutions to differentiate, so they can cater more adequately for individual needs. At the same time, accountability requirements are being strengthened, *e.g.* through the enhanced role of the independent Inspectorate of Education since 2002 (see www.minocw.nl/english_oud/guaran/). In 2005, primary education will be the last education sector to switch to a "lump-sum" based budgeting system. Policies targeted at reducing teacher shortages are focusing on a more proactive school role in human resources management, and substantial increases in teachers' salaries. New and shorter paths to the teaching profession are being created (see www.minocw.nl/arbeidsmarkt/babo90/). In vocational education, creating continuous learning pathways is the major issue in order to raise quality and decrease the number of early-school leavers (see www.minocw.nl/english_oud/bve/site/). In higher education, internationalisation is the crucial issue. As a result of the Bologna declaration, universities and institutions for higher vocational education are implementing the Bachelor/Master structure. Accreditation procedures in Dutch higher education are also being introduced (see www.nao-ho.nl).

NEW ZEALAND

New Zealand's education policy making is made at the national level, but individual institutions have local management autonomy (see www.minedu.govt.nz). In 2002 a ten-year Strategic Plan for Early Childhood Pathways to the Future, Ngā Huarahi Arataki, was released. At the plan's core are three goals: increase participation in early childhood education services; improve the quality of services; and promote collaborative relationships (see www.minedu.govt.nz). Tertiary education participation has expanded rapidly over the past decade. The Tertiary Education Strategy 2002-2007 sets out a five-year approach for a more collaborative and co-operative tertiary system, contributing to national goals and more closely connected to enterprises and local communities. At least once every three years a Statement of Education Priorities (STEP) is to be published setting out the short- to medium-term priorities. A new entity, the Tertiary Education Commission was established with responsibility for implementation of government policy in the tertiary area [see www.minedu.govt.nz (Tertiary Education Reforms)]. At the beginning of 2002, Specialist

Education services, previously a separate crown entity providing services for students with special education needs, was integrated with the Ministry of Education [see *www.minedu.govt.nz* (Special Education)]. In 2002 the new standards-based national school qualifications system, the National Certificate of Educational Achievement (NCEA), was introduced (see *www.ncea.govt.nz*).

NORWAY

Education supervision in Norway is exercised by municipal authorities (compulsory education), county authorities (upper secondary education), and the Ministry of Education and Research (tertiary education). The Ministry has the ultimate responsibility for supervision of education (except for pre-school provision) (see *www.dep.no/archive/ ufdvedlegg/01/04/utdan021.pdf*). In 2002-2003 higher education – both private and public – is being reformed (termed the Quality Reform) (see *www.dep.no/archive/ufdvedlegg/01/02/thequ067.pdf*). The main elements are greater autonomy for institutions, a more result-oriented funding formula, the establishment of a new independent agency for quality assurance (see *www.nokut.no*), and increased international co-operation. Academic courses will now be more structured, with regular guidance and monitoring of each student. A new structure with Bachelor/Master/PhD degrees is being introduced, in line with the Bologna process. In parallel to this reform the system of financial support to students has been improved. Ongoing reforms in primary and secondary education aim to improve quality by giving more autonomy to schools, and by securing more knowledge and openness regarding educational outcomes. Reforms include developing a national system for quality evaluation and development; establishing a new system for financing independent/private schools; simplifying rules and regulations; and re-organising the national education administration. The school reforms will be principally implemented during 2003-2005.

PORTUGAL

Portugal is a unitary political system where the administration of education is largely centralised, with the major exception of the autonomous regions of the Madeira and Açores. In April 2002 a new Government was elected, and the main goal of its educational programme is "To invest in the qualification of the Portuguese people" (see *www.min-edu.pt*). The sector corresponding to higher education has been integrated in the Ministry for Science and Higher Education (see *www.mces.gov.pt*). Legislation on the development and quality assurance of higher education has been introduced. The Ministry of Education has been reorganised. A key element has been the creation of the new Directorate-General for Vocational Training, with the aim of integrating the lifelong education and training policies and systems. In 2002 legislation on the Evaluation System for Non-Higher Education was introduced to promote school self-evaluation and external evaluation. To strengthen the decentralisation of educational responsibility to the local level a new law concerning the Educational Municipal Councils and the Educational Charter has also been adopted.

SPAIN

Spain is a state, politically and administratively, structured in Regional Governments. The Regional Governments have responsibility for education. As such, it is difficult to provide a short summary of major education policy developments. However, Constitution provides that the State has the authority to establish the broad structure of the education system and the basic common curricula. Substantial reforms in these areas have been underway since 2000. In 2002 two key pieces of legislation were passed, which are being implemented by the Ministry of Education, Culture and Sports: the Act on Qualifications and Vocational Training; and the Act on Quality in Education. These Acts aim at modernising the education and training systems, lifting quality, and introducing greater flexibility and responsiveness to social and economic change. For further information see *www.mecd.es*

UNITED KINGDOM

The United Kingdom is a parliamentary democracy with a constitutional monarch as head of State. There is no one educational system in the United Kingdom, and there are important differences in curricula and examinations between England, Northern Ireland, Scotland and Wales. The Department for Education and Skills (DfES) has responsibility for early years and childcare, schools and lifelong learning in England (see *www.dfes.gov.uk*). For 2003 the Government highlighted three areas of focus: truancy; secondary reform; and a review of higher education. The 2003 DfES document, A *New Specialist System: Transforming Secondary Education*, sets out the main themes for reforming secondary education (see *www.teachernet.gov.uk/makingadiff*). In early 2003, the Government also published 14-19: *opportunity and excellence* setting out the vision to transform the learning experience for young people, so that they are more motivated and have a commitment to continued learning, whether in school, college or the labour force (see *www.dfes.gov.uk/14-19greenpaper*). A 2003 strategy document, *The Future of Higher Education*, sets out the 10-year vision for development of higher education (see *www.dfes.gov.uk/highereducation/hestrategy*). National priorities for higher education in the next decade in Scotland are documented in *The Higher Education Review Phase 2: A Framework for Higher Education in Scotland* (see *www.scotland.gov.uk/library5/lifelong/herp2-00.asp*).

UNITED STATES

The United States has a federal political system. Education policy making is shared between the federal government (which provides general policy guidance, support for special programmes and research, and enforcement of equal access laws), the States (which regulate the schools) and local school districts (which operate the schools) (see *www.ed.gov/NLE/USNEI/us/inst-geninfo*). Enactment of the *No Child Left Behind Act* in early 2002 was a major step to strengthen primary and secondary schools. This law makes federal funding to States contingent on the States' requiring their local school districts to: undertake annual testing in reading and mathematics for students in grades three to eight; make available public information about how well students achieve; assure improvement in student achievement for all groups; give parents options to remove their children from schools that do not improve; strengthen early reading programmes; and tap new sources of talented teachers through recruitment incentives, loan forgiveness and tax relief for teachers (see *www.ed.gov*). Improving early reading programmes is a special priority. This effort aims to raise the calibre and quality of classroom instruction; base instruction on scientifically proven methods; and provide professional training for educators in reading instruction (see *www.ed.gov/about/offices/list/oese*).

EDUCATION POLICY ANALYSIS
Purposes and previous editions

The *Education Policy Analysis* series was launched by the OECD in 1996. It forms part of the work programme of the OECD Education Committee, and responds to the policy priorities established by OECD Education Ministers. The series is prepared by the Education and Training Division of the OECD Directorate for Education.

Purposes

The main purposes of *Education Policy Analysis* are:

- To assist education policy-makers and others concerned with education policy to make better decisions by drawing on international and comparative work;
- To draw out the key insights and policy implications arising from OECD education activities, international data and indicators, and related studies; and
- To present findings, analyses and discussion in a succinct and accessible form.

Education Policy Analysis is produced annually (except in 2000, when a special edition was prepared for the 2001 OECD Education Ministerial meeting).

Contents of the previous editions

2002
- Chapter 1 Strengthening early childhood programmes: a policy framework
- Chapter 2 Improving both quality and equity: insights from PISA 2000
- Chapter 3 The teaching workforce: concerns and policy challenges
- Chapter 4 The growth of cross-border education
- Chapter 5 Rethinking human capital

2001
- Chapter 1 Lifelong learning for all: policy directions
- Chapter 2 Lifelong learning for all: taking stock
- Chapter 3 Closing the gap: securing benefits for all from education and training
- Chapter 4 Competencies for the knowledge economy
- Chapter 5 What future for our schools?

1999
- Chapter 1 Resources for lifelong learning: what might be needed and how might it be found?
- Chapter 2 Early childhood education and care: getting the most from the investment
- Chapter 3 Technology in education: trends, investment, access and use
- Chapter 4 Tertiary education: extending the benefits of growth to new groups

1998
- Chapter 1 Lifelong learning: a monitoring framework and trends in participation
- Chapter 2 Teachers for tomorrow's schools
- Chapter 3 Supporting youth pathways
- Chapter 4 Paying for tertiary education: the learner perspective

1997
- Chapter 1 Expenditures on education
- Chapter 2 Lifelong investment in human capital
- Chapter 3 Literacy skills: use them or lose them
- Chapter 4 Failure at school: patterns and responses
- Chapter 5 Responding to new demand in tertiary education

1996
- Chapter 1 An overview of enrolment and expenditure trends
- Chapter 2 Education outcomes: measuring student achievement and adult competence
- Chapter 3 Transition from school to work
- Chapter 4 Teachers' pay and conditions

ALSO AVAILABLE

Education at a Glance: OECD Indicators 2003 (2003)
Beyond Rhetoric: Adult Learning Policies and Practices (2003)
Financing Education – Investments and Returns: Analysis of the World Education Indicators 2002 (2003)
Schooling for Tomorrow – Networks of Innovation: Towards New Models for Managing Schools and Systems (2003)
New Challenges for Educational Research (2003)
Measuring Knowledge Management in the Business Sector: First Steps (2003)
Disability in Higher Education (2003)

Programme for International Student Assessment (PISA)

Literacy Skills for the World of Tomorrow: Further Results from PISA 2000 (2003)
The PISA 2003 Assessment Framework: Mathematics, Reading, Science and Problem-Solving Knowledge and Skills (2003)
Learners for Life: Student Approaches to Learning: Results from PISA 2000 (2003)
Student Engagement at School – A Sense of Belonging and Participation (2003)

Reviews of National Policies for Education

Reviews of National Policies for Education – Polytechnic Education in Finland (2003)
Reviews of National Policies for Education – Tertiary Education in Switzerland (2003)
Reviews of National Policies for Education – Bulgaria (2003)
Reviews of National Policies for Education – South Eastern Europe (2 volumes) (2003)

For further information: www.oecd.org/edu

OECD PUBLICATIONS, 2, rue André-Pascal, 75775 PARIS CEDEX 16
PRINTED IN FRANCE
(96 2003 12 1 P 1) ISBN 92-64-10455-0 – No. 53203 2003